THE BERKELEY SERIES IN AMERICAN HISTORY

The Secession Crisis, 1860-1861

Edited by

P. J. STAUDENRAUS

UNIVERSITY OF CALIFORNIA AT DAVIS

RAND McNALLY & COMPANY · CHICAGO

The Berkeley Series in American History
Charles Sellers, editor   Rand McNally

CONTENTS

INTRODUCTION

AMERICANS LIVING IN 1860–1861 WITNESSED THE COLLAPSE OF THE UNION under the Constitution and the failure of democratic methods to resolve sharp political disputes between the North and the South. The election of Abraham Lincoln on the Republican party ticket signaled a movement for disunion. During the agonizing "secession winter" seven southern states, beginning with South Carolina on December 20, 1860, hurriedly severed their political bonds with the Union. By early February, 1861, Mississippi, Florida, Alabama, Georgia, Louisiana, and Texas had followed South Carolina's action. Even before Lincoln took office, the cotton states had decided that peaceful secession and the creation of a southern confederacy were preferable to remaining in the Union under a president elected by a northern party. Thus arose a crisis unparalleled in American history. Its resolution came only after four years of disastrous civil war.

The secessionist movement climaxed many years of earnest debate over the nature of the Union, state sovereignty, state rights, and the authority of the federal government. The debate had turned on many issues, including tariffs, territorial expansion, regulation of slave property in the territories, rendition of fugitive slaves, and proposals to reopen the African slave trade. Though southern politicians had frequently threatened secession as the ultimate solution to all disputes, few men believed the threats to be genuine, for, despite its minority position, the South had succeeded in obtaining concessions on virtually all issues. Congress had enacted a stronger fugitive slave law and repealed the Missouri compromise restriction on slavery extension in the territories. The Supreme Court had asserted the right of slave property to enter all federal territories. Moreover, until 1861 the executive branch of the government had rested in the hands of southern men or their friends. When secession actually came in 1860–1861, many Americans were incredulous. Northern men could not believe that southern states really meant to disrupt the Union. Skepticism gradually turned to alarm. By the time Lincoln entered office, northern men had weighed the value of Union and concluded that separation was neither constitutional nor possible, and southern men had concluded that separation was necessary and irrevocable.

The materials presented here are selected to help evaluate the causes of the secession crisis and the alternatives proposed by the opponents of disunion. The following questions may help to guide your reading of the speeches, articles, letters, and messages.

I. What did the South expect to obtain from secession that it could not obtain within the Union?

II. What arguments did the secessionists use to justify breaking up the Union, and what were the merits of their case?

III. Was there a conspiracy to destroy the Union?

IV. Why was northern opinion slow to develop?

V. How did Lincoln's views of secession differ from Buchanan's?

WAS SECESSION A CONSPIRACY OR

A POPULAR MOVEMENT?

To LOVERS OF THE UNION, THE RAPID-FIRE WITHDRAWAL OF SEVEN STATES appeared to be the result of careful planning and coordination. Before, during, and after the Civil War, writers charged that a few disgruntled southern politicians, using any pretext available, had conspired to destroy the Union. Whether the secession crisis was in fact the work of conspirators seeking to impose their will on the silent masses of the South or the result of a powerful popular movement that overwhelmed Union sentiment is a question of historical interest, for men like Abraham Lincoln, William Henry Seward, and Stephen A. Douglas did *not* believe that the great majority of the southern people were disunionists at heart. Upon that belief they acted. Both viewpoints are presented in the following selections. Which writer makes the best case? Which offers the more plausible explanation? What constitutes a conspiracy? What is the evidence for a popular movement?

A.

CONSPIRACY

⟨John G. Nicolay, former private secretary to President Lincoln and Lincoln's biographer, concluded that the secession movement was the product of a conspiracy. (John G. Nicolay, *The Outbreak of Rebellion* [New York, 1881], pp. 1–16.)⟩

THE FIFTH day of October, 1860, is the initial point of the American Rebellion. Its conception, animus, and probably its plans, lay much farther back. It had been seriously proposed once or twice before, but it was then that its formal organization was begun. On that day Governor Gist, of South Carolina, wrote a confidential circular letter, which he dispatched by the hand of a special messenger, to the governors of what were commonly designated the Cotton States. In this letter he asked an interchange of opinions which he might be at liberty to submit to a consultation of leading men of South Carolina. He said South Carolina would unquestionably call a convention as soon as it was ascertained that a majority of Lincoln electors were chosen in the then pending presidential election. "If a single State secedes," he said, "she will follow her. If no other State takes the lead, South Carolina will secede (in my opinion) alone, if she has any assurance that she will be soon followed by another or other States; otherwise it is doubtful." He asked information, and advised concerted action.

North Carolina was first to respond. The people would not, so wrote the governor under date of October 18th, consider Lincoln's election a sufficient cause for disunion, and the Legislature would probably not call a convention. The Governor of Alabama, under date of October 25th, thought Alabama would not secede alone, but would secede in cooperation with two or more States. The Governor of Mississippi, under date of October 26th, wrote: "If any State moves, I think Mississippi will go with her." On the same day the Governor of Louisiana answered: "I shall not advise the secession of my State, and I will add that I do not think the people of Louisiana will ultimately decide in favor of that course." The Governor of Georgia, under date of October 31st, advocated retaliatory legislation, and ventured his opinion that the people of Georgia would wait for some overt act. Florida alone responded with anything like enthusiasm, but only after the lapse of a month. Her governor said that Florida was "ready to wheel into line with the gallant Palmetto State, or any other Cotton State or States," and thought she would unquestionably call a convention.

The discouraging tone of these answers established, beyond controversy, that, excepting in South Carolina, the rebellion was not in any sense a popular revolution, but was a conspiracy among the prominent local office-holders and politicians, which the people neither expected nor desired, and which they were made eventually to justify and uphold by the usual arts and expedients of conspiracy.

Directly and indirectly, the South had practically controlled the government during its whole existence. Excited to ambition by this success, she sought to perpetuate that control. The extension of slavery and the creation of additional Slave States was a necessary step in the scheme, and became the well-defined single issue in the presidential election. But in this contest the South for the first time met overwhelming defeat. The choice of Lincoln was a conclusive and final decision, in legal form and by constitutional majorities, that slavery should not be extended; and the popular vote of 1860 transferred the balance of power irrevocably to the Free States.

In the political discussions throughout this presidential campaign, as well as in preceding years, the South had made free and loud use of two leading arguments, always with telling effect: the first, to intimidate the North, was the threat of disunion; the second, to "fire the Southern heart," was the entirely unfounded alarm-cry that the North, if successful, would not merely exclude slavery from federal territories, but would also destroy slavery in the Slave States. The unthinking masses of the South accepted both these arguments in their literal sense; and Southern public opinion, excited and suspicious, became congenial soil in which the intended revolt easily took root.

The State of South Carolina, in addition, had been little else than a school of treason for thirty years. She was, moreover, peculiarly adapted to become the hotbed of conspiracy by the fact that of all the States she was least republican in both the character of her people and the form of her institutions. She was exclusive, aristocratic, reactionary; had a narrow distrust of popular participation in government, and longed for the distinctions of caste and privilege in society.

It would seem that, before the governors' replies were all received, the consultation or caucus for which they were solicited was held, and the programme of insurrection agreed upon. Circumstances rendered a special session of the South Carolina Legislature necessary. The election was held during the month of October. Local fanaticism tolerated no opposition party in the State, and under the manipulation of the conspirators the prevailing question was, who was the most zealous "resistance" candidate. To a legislature elected from this kind of material, Governor Gist, on November 5th, sent a defiant, revolutionary message —the first official notice and proclamation of insurrection. He declared that "our institutions" were in danger from the hostility of the "fixed majorities" of the North; and recommended the calling of a State convention, and the purchase of arms and material of war.

A lingering doubt about the result of the presidential contest appears in the formal choice by the Legislature, of electors who would vote for Breckinridge and Lane. But that doubt was short-lived. The morning of November 7th brought the certain news of the election of Lincoln and Hamlin on the previous day, and the rejoicings which would have been uttered over their defeat became jubilations that their success offered the long-coveted pretext for disunion.

From this time forth everything was managed to swell the revolutionary furor. The Legislature immediately ordered a convention, made appropriations, passed military bills. The federal officeholders, with much public flourish of their patriotic sacrifice, resigned their offices. Military companies enrolled themselves in the city; organizations of minute-men sprang up in the rural neighborhoods. Drills, parades, meetings, bonfires, secession harangues, secession cockades, palmetto flags, purchase of fire-arms and powder, singing of the Marseillaise— there is not room to enumerate the follies to which the general populace, especially of Charleston, devoted their days and nights. There was universal satisfaction: to the conspirators, because their schemes were progressing; to the rabble, because it had a continuous holiday.

Amid unflagging excitement of this character, which received a daily stimulus from similar proceedings beginning and growing in other Cotton States, November and the first half of December passed away. Meanwhile, a new governor, Francis W. Pickens, a revolutionist of a yet more radical type than his predecessor, was chosen by the Legislature and inaugurated, and the members of the Convention authorized by the Legislature were chosen at an election held on December 6th. The South Carolina Convention met at Columbia, the capital of the State, according to appointment, on December 17, 1860, but, on account of a local epidemic, at once adjourned to Charleston. That body was, like the Legislature, the immediate outgrowth of the current conspiracy, and doubtless counted many of the conspirators among its members. It therefore needed no time to make up its mind. On the fourth day of its term it passed unanimously what it called an Ordinance of Secession, in the following words:

"We, the people of the State of South Carolina, in convention assembled, do declare and ordain, and it is hereby declared and ordained, that the ordinance adopted by us in convention on the 23d day of May, in the year of our Lord 1788, whereby the Constitution of the United States of America was ratified, and also all Acts and parts of Acts of the General Assembly of this State ratifying amendments of the said Constitution, are hereby repealed; and that the Union now subsisting between South Carolina and other States, under the name of the United States of America, is hereby dissolved."

. . . The Ordinance of Secession of South Carolina was passed in secret session, a little after mid-day, on December 20th. The fact was immediately made public by huge placards issued from the Charleston printing-offices; and by special direction of the convention, the event was further celebrated by firing guns, ringing bells, and other jubilations. To carry this studied theatrical effect to its fullest extent, a session of the convention was held that same night, to which the members marched in procession, where the formal signing of the Ordinance was sought to be magnified into a solemn public ceremony; after which the chairman proclaimed South Carolina an "independent commonwealth." With all the affectation of legality, formality, and present justification, some of the members were honest enough to acknowledge the true character of the event as the culmination of a chronic conspiracy, not a spontaneous revolution. "The secession of South Carolina," said one of the chief actors, "is not an event of a day. It is not anything produced by Mr. Lincoln's election, or by the non-execution of the Fugitive Slave Law. It is a matter which has been gathering head for thirty years." This, with many similar avowals, crowns and completes the otherwise abundant proof that the revolt was not only against right, but that it was without cause.

The original suggestion of Governor Gist in his circular letter, for a concerted insurrection, fell upon fruitful soil. The events which occurred in South Carolina were in substance duplicated in the neighboring States of Georgia, Florida, Alabama, Mississippi, and Louisiana. These States, however, had stronger and more formidable union minorities than South Carolina; or rather, if the truth could have been ascertained with safety, they had each of them decided majorities averse to secession, as was virtually acknowledged by their governors' replies to the Gist circular. But during the presidential campaign, the three Southern parties, for factional advantage, had vied with each other in their denunciations of the hated "Black Republicans"—they had berated each other as "submissionists" in secret league or sympathy with the Abolitionists. The partisans of Breckinridge—generally either active or latent disunionists—were ready, positive, and relentlessly aggressive; the adherents of Bell and of Douglas were demoralized and suspicious.

When Lincoln's election was, so unexpectedly to many, rendered certain, they could not recover in time to evade the searching question which the conspirators immediately thrust at them, "whether they would submit to Black Republican rule." A false shame and the inexorable tyranny of Southern public opinion made many a voter belie the honest convictions of his heart, and answer No, when at the very least he would gladly have evaded the inquiry.

The prominent office-holders, governors, senators, congressmen, judges, formed in each State a central clique of conspiracy. The governors had official authority to issue proclamations, to convene legislatures, to call out and command such militia as existed. Had their authority been wielded in behalf of the Union, no general revolt would have been possible; but, exercised without scruple or rest to promote secession, insurrection began with an official prestige which swept the hesitating and the timid irresistibly into the vortex of treason. Even then it was only by persistent nursing, management, and in many cases sheer deceit that a semblance of majorities was obtained to justify and apparently indorse the conspirators' plots. Legislatures were convened, commissioners sent from State to State, conventions called, military bills passed, minute-men and volunteer companies organized. Deliberative bodies were harangued by the conspirators' emissaries, and showered with inflammatory telegrams. After the meeting of Congress the fire-eaters of Washington held almost nightly caucuses, and sent addresses, solicitations, and commands from the capital. Individual opinion was overawed; the government was not only silent, but constantly yielding; legislative deliberation became, in secret session, legislative intrigue; pretexts were invented to defer and omit all proper scrutiny of election returns. The "State" was the idol of the hour. "The State commands" was as despotic a formula as "The king commands"; and the voter's personal judgment, the very basis and life-giving principle of republics, was obliterated between the dread of proscription and the blighting mildew of the doctrine of supreme State allegiance.

Certain features of the struggle deserve special explanation. The "irrepressible conflict" between North and South, between freedom and slavery, was not confined to the two sides of Mason and Dixon's line; it found a certain expression even in the Cotton States themselves. Most of these States embrace territory of a radically different quality. Their southern and sea-coast front is a broad belt of sea-islands, marshes, river-swamps, and low alluvial lands, exceedingly unhealthy from malarial fevers in the hot season, but of unsurpassed fertility, and possessing the picturesque aspects of an exuberant half-tropical vegetation. This is the region of the great cotton, rice, and sugar plantations which have made the South rich and famous; here the St. Clairs and Legrees of real life counted their slaves by hundreds, and aspired to sybaritic lives in ample, hospitable mansions, surrounded by magnificent and venerable live-oak and magnolia groves, avenues of stately palms, princely gardens of native and exotic bloom, and illimitable hedge-lines of the Cherokee rose; a swarm of house-servants to minister to pampered indolence and dispense a lavish hospitality; a troop of field-hands to fill the cotton, rice or sugar houses; a blending of Arcadian simplicity and feudal pretension; every plantation with its indulgent master, its exacting overseer, its submissive slaves. These were the lights of the picture; abler pens have painted the horrible background of bloody slave-whips, barbarous slave-codes, degrading slave-auctions, yellow fever, cypress-swamps, the bloodhound hunt, and the ever-present dread of servile insurrection. From such surroundings came the morbid dreams of an unholy league between perpetual bondage and free trade, which should rear a gigantic slave empire, before which the intellect, the power, the splendor, and the government of all preceding ages and nations should fade and wane.

The northern half of the Cotton States was very different; here were thin, sandy uplands of meagre productiveness; monotonous forests of pine and scrub-oak, running again into the more varied and romantic scenery of the subsiding spurs of the Alleghanies, blue crags, bright streams, shining waterfalls, and the changing, deciduous foliage of the North. Great slave-plantations could not flourish here; white population predominated; agriculture was varied; the husbandman had a sterner struggle with nature; and communities were burdened with all the economic and social detriments of the slave system, having none of its delights.

A dense slave population and ultra secessionism were, therefore, the rule in the southern, and white majorities and union feeling in the northern districts of the Cotton States. Therefore, also, political power lay in the slave region, which again was allied to the commercial interests clustering about southern seaports. All the leverage was in the hands of treason—offices, ostracism, advantage in representation, commercial ambition, party ascendancy. The wonder is, not that secession succeeded in the struggle, but that there was any serious contest at all. With all this, there is strong ground for belief that insurrection gained its ends at last only through chicane, deceit, and fraud. Not a single Cotton State but Texas dared to submit its Ordinance of Secession to a direct vote of the people.

The struggle assumed its most determined phase in Georgia. She was the Empire State of the South, and, therefore, indispensable to the conspiracy, in which distinguished citizens of hers—Governor Brown, Secretary Cobb, Senators Toombs and Iverson, and others—were conspicuous ring-leaders. The more rabid fire-eaters desired that the Legislature should at once pass an act of secession; Stephens and other conservatives opposed this course. "The Legislature were not elected for such a purpose," said he. "They came here to do their duty as legislators. They have sworn to support the Constitution of the United States. They did not come here to disrupt this government. I am, therefore, for submitting all these questions to a convention of the people." In due time a convention was called by unanimous vote of the Legislature. Then followed a spirited campaign to elect delegates. It early became evident that, while the people of Georgia were irritated to the point of demanding new guarantees for slavery, they were decidedly against disunion. Thereupon the conspirators invented a bold trick. "The truth is," explains Alexander H. Stephens, "in my judgment the wavering scale in Georgia was turned by a sentiment the key-note to which was given in the words, 'We can make better terms out of the Union than in it.' . . . This one idea did more, in my opinion, in carrying the State out, than all the arguments and eloquence of all others combined. Two-thirds at least of those who voted for the Ordinance of Secession, did so, I have but little doubt, with a view to a more certain reformation of the Union." The heresy of supreme State allegiance was, however, the final and all-conquering engine of treason. Mr. Stephens himself, in his memorable speech in defence of the Union, is the striking illustration of Gulliver helpless in the cobwebs of Lilliput. To secede, he declared, was to break the Constitution. Good faith required the South to abide the election in peace. Lincoln could do her no harm against an adverse House and Senate. He adjured them not to rashly try the experiment of change; for liberty, once lost, might never be restored. These were words of sober wisdom, and, fearlessly adhered to by a few firm men, they might have paralyzed the revolt. Yet in the same speech he declared that, if Georgia seceded, he should bow to the will of her people—in other words, break the Constitution, break faith, and lose liberty. On this "easy descent" Georgia slid to her ruin. Under such examples the convention passed the secession ordinance, 208 to 89.

While thus in the States of South Carolina, Georgia, Alabama, Florida, Mississippi, and Louisiana, the conspiracy made pretentious efforts to clothe rebellion in the robes of law, and hide it behind the shield of constitutional forms, it pursued an altogether bold and unblushing course of usurpation in the State of Texas. The famous and somewhat eccentric General Houston was governor. His own long struggle to bring Texas into the Union made him loth to join in its destruction. He resisted the secession conspiracy; but his southern pro-slavery prejudices also imbued him with the prevalent antagonism to the Republican party. He therefore nursed a scheme to carry Texas back into independent sovereignty, and, with her territory and population as a basis, to undertake the conquest and annexation of Mexico.

But the conspirators, ignoring all restraint, without a shadow of legality, assembled a revolutionary State convention, and on February 1st passed an ordinance of secession, with a provision submitting it to a popular vote. Houston, pursuing his side intrigue, approved a joint resolution of the State Legislature (February 4th) to legalize the convention, but accompanied his approval with a protest that it should have no effect except to elicit public decision on the single question of adherence to the Union. When in due time an alleged vote (taken on February 23d) ratifying the ordinance was submitted to him, he refused to recognize further acts of the convention; whereupon the enraged convention (March 16th) declared his office vacant, and empowered the lieutenant-governor to seize the executive authority. . . .

But the mere perversion of elections, the adoption of a secession ordinance, and the assumption of independent authority, was not enough for the Cotton Republics. Though they hoped to evade civil war by shrewd intrigue, they well understood they had no certain immunity from it. It was therefore essential to possess the arms and military posts within their borders. There were in the seceded States one quite extensive navy-yard, at Pensacola, Florida; twelve to fifteen harbor-forts along the Atlantic and Gulf coasts, capable of mounting a thousand guns, and having cost over five millions; half a dozen arsenals, containing an aggregate of one hundred and fifteen thousand arms, transferred there from northern arsenals by Secretary Floyd about a year before, on pretence of danger from slave insurrections. In addition there were three mints, four important custom-houses, three revenue-cutters on duty at the several seaports, and a variety of other miscellaneous property. This estimate does not include the . . . public property surrendered by General Twiggs in Texas, which of itself formed an aggregate of eighteen military posts and stations, and arms and stores to a large amount and value.

This property had been purchased with the money of the Federal government; the land on which the buildings stood, though perhaps in some instances donated, was vested in the United States, not only by the right of eminent domain, but also by formal legislative deeds of cession from the States themselves.

It is now assumed that the heresy of State supremacy, through which the States pretended to derive their authority to pass secession ordinances, also restored to them the right of eminent domain, or that they had always retained it; that therefore they might, under the law of nations, justifiably take possession, holding themselves responsible in money damages to be settled by negotiation. The hypothesis and its parent dogma were of course both false and absurd. The Government of the United States, unlike other great nations, has steadily opposed the maintenance of a large military force in time of peace. The whole regular army amounted to only a little over seventeen thousand men. These, as usual, were mainly occupied in defence of the western frontier against hostile Indian tribes. Consequently, but three of these southern forts were garrisoned, and they by only about a company each. An equal force was stationed for the protection of the arsenals at Augusta, Ga., Mt. Vernon, Ala., and Baton Rouge, La.

As a necessary part of the conspiracy, the governors of the Cotton States now, by official order to their extemporized militia companies, took forcible possession of these forts, arsenals, navy-yard, custom-houses, and other property, in many cases even before their secession ordinances were passed. This was nothing less than levying actual war against the United States, though as yet attended by no violence or bloodshed. . . .

B.

POPULAR MOVEMENT

¶Professor Ralph A. Wooster of Lamar State College of Technology, Beaumont, Texas, recently surveyed the secession movement from the vantage point of one hundred years. He argues that secession had broad popular support. (Ralph A. Wooster, "The Secession of the Lower South: An Examination of Changing Interpretations," Civil War History [June 1961], VII, 117–27.)]

FROM THE moment South Carolina first took the road to disunion historians have discussed the nature of the secession movement in the states of the lower South. Much of the early discussion focused on the question of whether or not the secession of these states was the result of a conspiracy on the part of a few Southern officeholders and slaveholders, who succeeded by a skillful combination of demagoguery and deception in overriding the wishes of the people and carrying their states out of the Union. This belief that Southern leaders conspired to divide the Union was popular in the North throughout the Civil War. It became, as Thomas J. Pressly has said, the "well-nigh universal theme in the Unionists histories." . . . The image was created of Southern slaveholders and political leaders plotting the destruction of the Union long before the presidential election of 1860. The breakup of the Democratic party and the subsequent election of a Republican administration were the work of these conspirators, who thus assured the secession of the slaveholding states. . . .

This question of *who* supported secession is quite important to an understanding of the movement in the lower South. Was it only a minority group as maintained by the early unionist writers, or was it actually a majority of the people in the lower South? In refuting the conspiracy thesis James Ford Rhodes treated secession as a popular movement of the Southern people, a position that has won wide acceptance among twentieth-century scholars, including Dwight L. Dumond, Clement Eaton, and E. Merton Coulter. Dumond, who wrote the most scholarly general treatment of the secession movement, felt that the secessionists had a working majority in all the states of the lower South and that the opposition to secession in the winter of 1860–61 was principally over the methods of separation. Eaton, author of two widely used textbooks of Southern history, noted that emotionalism encouraged by agitators helped to sweep the people along; he added that the wave of rejoicing which followed the passage of the secession ordinances indicated a deep popular approval. And Professor Coulter observed that outside of a few very wealthy and a few extremely poor all sections of the lower South favored separate state action in 1861.

The above views have not been accepted by all contemporary scholars. Outstanding in his opposition to these views is David M. Potter. While not advocating the old conspiracy thesis of secession, Potter does express the view that secession was unpopular not only in the upper and border slaveholding states but in the lower South as well. He stated:

> Furthermore secession was not basically desired even by a majority in the lower South, and the secessionists succeeded less because of the intrinsic popularity of their program than because of the extreme skill with which they utilized an emergency psychology, the promptness with which they invoked unilateral action by individual states, and the firmness with which they refused to submit the question of secession to popular referenda. . . .

The contention of Potter that the majority of people in the lower South did not support secession is . . . based upon four main points: (1) the appreciable decline in number of people participating in the election for convention delegates compared to the total vote in the November presidential vote; (2) the shortness of the period for canvassing and campaigning; (3) the strength of the opposition to secession in all conventions with the exception of South Carolina, Mississippi, and Texas; and (4) except in the case of Texas, the non-submission of the work of the conventions to popular referendum.

A study of the secession movement in the individual states of the lower South reveals a number of weaknesses in the above contentions. The decline in the number of votes between the presidential election and the elections for convention delegates, for example, cannot be attributed simply to opposition to separate state action. To many Southerners in 1860–61, secession was an accomplished fact even before the election of convention delegates; some of them therefore did not bother to participate in what they regarded to be a *fait accompli*. In his *Secession Movement in Alabama*, Clarence P. Denman noted that eighteen counties in that state were carried by a vote of 90 per cent or more of the total and that, since the vote in most of these counties was very small in comparison with that cast in the presidential election, it can only be inferred that a considerable number of people had not troubled themselves to vote because they were confident of the outcome. Many counties in Georgia, South Carolina, and Mississippi returned a light vote because the separate state action ticket was unopposed and its supporters were under no pressure to go to the polls. Too, in Georgia an extremely bad storm on election day reduced the vote cast for convention delegates. Obviously, to consider all the voters who failed to participate in the elections as antisecessionists is an oversimplification.

The criticism of the shortness of the period for canvassing and campaigning, the second point in Potter's argument, fails to take account of the exigencies of the situation in the winter and spring of 1860–61. Whether the South should remain in the Union upon certain conditions, or secede at once, was a decision that had to be made before Lincoln was inaugurated. Although some Southerners feared an overt act from the new administration, many more feared a subtle campaign to divide the South and to array non-slaveholders against slaveholders. Even conservative Southerners admitted the necessity of agreement upon some type of policy before that time. Moreover, the states of the lower South had previously given warnings that conventions would be called should Lincoln be elected. It is therefore difficult to sustain a charge that the convention elections were unduly hurried when four or five additional weeks were allowed for debating issues that had already been under discussion for a decade.

The contention that there was strong opposition to secession in nearly all of the conventions would not stand alone, nor do its proponents intend it to do so. Instead, they maintain that such a powerful opposition within the conventions despite threats and intimidation if reinforced by the opposition which refused to participate in the elections, amounted to a majority of the inhabitants of the various Southern states. A principal fallacy in this line of argument is the assumption that the organized opposition in the conventions of the cotton states was predominantly unionist. Such an assumption is in many cases erroneous. With the exception of the Texas convention, where only eight members voted against secession, the opposition to separate state secession in the lower South was mainly centered on the principle of "cooperation," which to part of its supporters meant cooperative action by the slave states to secure their rights either in or out of the Union as events might dictate. To others it means simply secession from the Union, but *en masse*, and by concurrent action rather than by separate state action.

In two states, Mississippi and Louisiana, a majority of cooperationists belong to this second class; they were genuine secessionists who disagreed with the separate state actionists not over the need for but over the question of time and method of withdrawal. In Florida the cooperationists were a badly divided group, some favoring secession if Alabama or Georgia acted first, some favoring secession if approved by a vote of the people, and a few opposing any form of separation. Even in Alabama and Georgia many of the cooperationists were actually secessionists, but felt that a last united effort should be made to compromise. Comparatively few Alabamians and Georgians of 1861 were unconditional unionists desiring to stay in the Union at all costs. Nor were a majority of the "conditional unionists" present in the conventions "submissionists." Certainly the conditional unionists were opposed to immediate separation from the Union, and in that respect were more conservative than the cooperationists proper; but only a few favored remaining in the Union at any cost. Even if we consider all conditional unionists as opposed to secession at any time—though in fact a majority of this group favored secession should guarantees from the North not be forthcoming—their strength was slight.

The failure of the conventions to submit their work to a popular referendum may be explained by the fact that the delegates regarded such a procedure as not only costly and time-consuming but also as entirely unnecessary. The delegates were fresh from the people, having been chosen only a few weeks before, and knew the will of the people. As James G. Randall has pointed out, the referendum was not part of the Southerner's time-honored theories on secession; the only instrument in the secession procedure was the constituent convention such as was elected in each state of the lower South.

Thus the aforementioned contentions that a minority group carried secession seem open to question. That there was opposition to immediate separation both within and without the conventions is true; that this opposition was equal to the secessionist strength is not. And once the conventions had acted in favor of immediate secession the public generally accorded its approval. The bulk of contemporary accounts from both secessionists and unionist sources testify to the joyful reception accorded the news that the conventions had acted for secession. Insofar as public display of enthusiasm and zeal can be taken as a true measure of the feelings of a people, Southerners in 1860–61 favored the ordinances of separation. Rightly or wrongly, the majority of people in the lower South were convinced that their hopes lay not within but without the Union. From South Carolina on the Atlantic to Texas on the Gulf, party ties and labels were forgotten; the lower South was at last united.

THE ARGUMENT FOR SECESSION

THE SECESSION CRISIS OF 1860–1861 CAME AT THE END OF A DECADE OF agitation by a minority of vocal, determined, and persuasive southern politicians and publicists. In 1850 a few men had boldly advocated secession as the only solution to the problems and controversies arising out of the conquest of Mexico and the subsequent annexation of a large portion of her lands. The earlier secession movement collapsed when Georgia refused to follow the lead of South Carolina, Alabama, and Mississippi and persuaded the cotton states to accept the "Georgia Platform of 1850" which avowed that the South had made its last concessions on such questions as the extension of slavery into western territories, the return of fugitive slaves, and the future of slavery in the District of Columbia. Through the 1850's, secessionists like William L. Yancey of Alabama, Robert Barnwell Rhett of South Carolina, and Edmund Ruffin of Virginia bided their time, occasionally charging that the northern states were subverting the Constitution and invalidating the Union.

A.

WILLIAM L. YANCEY, "APOSTLE OF DISUNION"

⟨After 1851, Yancey recognized that for the time being secession was a dead issue, but in speeches and letters he argued that the time would eventually come when the South would concede no more to northern demands. The following selection is from a speech delivered at Columbus, Georgia, in 1855. (John W. DuBose, *The Life and Times of William Lowndes Yancey* [1892; reprinted New York: P. Smith, 1942], I, 297–303.)

Why did Yancey disavow national parties? What was the alternative to secession? What advantages did Yancey expect from secession? Why did he believe the South would eventually espouse disunion?⟩

FELLOW CITIZENS: . . . As is well known to you, I have for several years stood aloof from the contests of the old national parties which have divided the people of the South, believing that their tendency has been in direct antagonism to a true Southern policy. This conviction has been strengthened, not weakened, by late events; and I verily believe that a like conviction had been growing up in the minds of the Southern people, since the passage of those measures known as the compromise acts of 1850; that they were beginning to realize, and to act upon the belief, that to their union upon some common policy alone could they look for ultimate protection within or safety out of the Union. It is an undeniable fact, that, since the contest in the South, consequent upon the passage of the compromise bills, there has been an unusual calmness and repose amongst our people. An indifferent observer might have attributed it to apathy—that apathy which often follows intense excitement. But to him who looked deeper into the great public heart, and who was at all familiar with the character of our patient, brave and self-reliant people, another aspect was presented —that of a people whose minds were made up on the great issues of the day, who were agreed upon the question of their wrongs, and upon the manner of their redress; and with no fears as to the result, were calmly awaiting the hour of action. It followed, necessarily, from this state of the public mind, that party ties sat loosely upon men—that tho' the old party organizations still existed, their members regarded their political opponents here at home with less of prejudice and hostility than had been their wont; that a spirit of enlarged charity, of patriotic brotherhood animated all. We were almost in view of that period, of the arrival of which many a patriot had gone to his grave despairing, in which, without distinction of party, there would be a union of the South for the sake of the South.

This state of things had been preceded by great differences of opinion as to the proper course to be pursued. A large part of the Southern people believed longer forbearance would not be a virtue; that no reasonable hope could be entertained that the North, with its numerical power, flushed with triumphs and animated with a fanatical zeal which laughed to scorn the Bible and the Constitution, would respect that compromise, or cease its assaults upon us; and thus believing urged upon the Southern States an immediate secession from the Union. They argued that the federal government had ceased to be a protection to Southern Rights—that it had become a powerful machinery in the hands of the North to aggrandize itself at the expense of the South. The great mass of our fellow citizens, however, more patient and more hopeful, determined against the immediate secession policy. They resolved that they would acquiesce in the compromise measures as a final adjustment of the slavery issues, and would resist, to the last extremity, any further aggression upon the South. In one State—the State of Georgia—this resolve was made its fundamental law, and I believe I am fully justified in saying that the majority of every other Southern State, or, at least every cotton State, acquiesced in the policy indicated by Georgia. The minority, consisting of the immediate Secessionists, were forced to yield, and, driven by this popular decision from their more advanced positions, naturally found their next resistance ground on the Georgia Platform. After that decision, there was no further disagreement in the South. All parties stood in alignment upon that position, animated by one resolve, aye, and with one faith in the future.

Far different was the condition of things at the North. That section was in strong contrast with the repose of the South. Tho' no right of theirs was even questioned, the public mind, like a great cauldron, seethed with all the elements of Abolition fanaticism. Whatever their differences of opinion in local matters, there was, for all practical purposes, unity of sentiment and unity of action on the slavery issue. They are united in pronouncing slavery a political and social evil. They are united in the sentiment that it would be a great political evil that the institution should spread itself over the Territories, and that new slave States should thus be formed. They are united in the belief that it is incumbent upon them to do all in their power to oppose the increase of slavery. Thus far, all parties at the North, practically, are in unison. Their disagreements commence with a policy and constitutional obligations. They agree that Congress has the power to abolish slavery in the District of Columbia; they disagree only as to the policy of such an act. An immense majority of them agree that Congress has the power to exclude slave immigration to the Territories; they disagree only as to the propriety of such Congressional action, south of the Missouri compromise line. They agree that slaveholders can be constitutionally excluded from settling in the Territories, while in a condition of Territorial pupilage; they disagree as to the proper mode of effecting our exclusion. One faction contends that it is the duty of Congress to exclude us by law; another contends that the squatters have the right to exclude us by a law of their own making. Another holds (and this is the doctrine of General Cass) that we cannot hold slaves in a Territory, without the law of the Territorial Legislature legalizing slavery, while the largest and most active portion contend that neither Congress nor the Territorial Legislature, nor the Convention called to frame a Constitution for the new State can authorize the existence of slavery in a Territory or in a new State.

Thus, you perceive, our assailants are united in all the essentials of antagonism to slavery; they only disagree as to some of the modes necessary to exclude it from the Territories. An immense majority agree that there is a power to exclude us from settlement in the Territories, and, as a consequence, from having any voice in framing the Constitutions of new States.

Amidst all this free soil agitation there exists but one party that, either in spirit or sentiment, manifests any disposition to stand by the South and the Constitution, and that is the Democratic party. The old National Whig party has been completely absorbed by free-soilism and its very name abandoned. Tho' the Democracy has not fallen to this estate, it is evident that but little more than a remnant remains of its once mighty majorities. Year by year and election succeeding election, show that the members and leaders of that party decrease; until now, there remains, I believe, about one dozen of its members in the two Houses of Congress, including General Cass and his followers.

The controlling element in all Northern elections, at this time, is, opposition to slavery and at every election, the ranks of Abolitionism are swelled by new accessions, and those of the Democracy reduced by defeat or defection. The result is, the majority of anti-slavery men, found in the House of Representatives, while the Senate but bides its time until the same power shall fill its seats with fit compeers of Holland, Wilson and Seward. Is no lesson to be drawn from a review of these facts? Is the mind of the South to be seduced with the hope that at another election a re-action will take place and the tide of fanaticism will be rolled back by reason and a regard for the Constitutional right of the institutions of the slave States? Or does not wisdom cry aloud to us to take care of ourselves? If the North comes to its senses, well. But, at all events, let us prepare for the contingency that this state of things is likely to go on and will soon be brought to bear practically upon the question of our equality in the Union. It is folly to blind our eyes to our true condition. We are in the midst of a mighty sectional contest; and in the recognition of that fact, we will find the solution of this united North against the South, and the South against the North. The laws of nature in their majesty stand out from the issue more imperative than the obligations due to national parties, or even to Constitutions. The checks and balances of our noble Constitution, it is true, were designed to keep down and to control all those sectional elements that have arisen in the States of the Union. The just observance of the State Rights creed, in the conduct of the general government, would effectually keep the sectional elements in control and, indeed, leave no opportunity for their display. But the spirit of consolidation, overriding the genius of our system and usurping the rights of States and dominating in concerns outside of the federal jurisdiction, brings to the surface those sectional antagonisms which naturally underlie great interests, built upon varied industrial conditions, founded on soil and climate.

The Creator has beautified the face of this Union with sectional features. Absorbing all minor sub-divisions, He has made the North and the South; the one the region of frost, ribbed in with ice and granite; the other baring its generous bosom to the sun and ever smiling under its influence. The climate, soil and productions of these two grand divisions of the land, have made the character of their inhabitants. Those who occupy the one are cool, calculating, enterprising, selfish and grasping; the inhabitants of the other, are ardent, brave and magnanimous, more disposed to give than to accumulate, to enjoy ease rather than to labor.

The institution of slavery, tho' recognized by the federal Constitution, in the representative and tax paying features of the government is, nevertheless, essentially sectional. It exists for the benefit of the South and is its chief source of wealth and power; and now in the hour of its peril, assailed by the great Northern antagonistic force, it must look to the South alone for protection.

I have been somewhat diffuse and elaborate in presenting the present attitude of the North and the South toward each other, but it has been necessary to my argument. I have shown that a contest rages between the sections on account of a sectional institution prevailing here. I have shown that our assailants occupy the vantage ground in the conflict; that their numerical majority is cemented by a gradual increase of their victories at the polls, covering a series of years; that their opponents in the South have given way before them. It is a simple question of time, when the North will have gained control of each and every department of the government—executive, legislative and judicial.

The question, then, naturally arises, what protection have we against the arbitrary course of this Northern majority? Considering the question as a Constitutional one, the answer is clear—our protection consists in the recognition of the great State Rights doctrine, which compels majorities to respect the rights of minorities. By that doctrine the States are co-equal in interest in the Territories and Congress is but their agent to govern for the benefit of all. Neither squatters or settlers in the Territories carry any inherent right to make laws there. Laws can only be made there by the act of Congress organizing the Territorial government, and the inhabitants, of course, can only acquire from Congress such rights of legislation as Congress may itself possess. As Congress can make no law excluding slavery from the Territory, it follows, that it cannot delegate any such law making authority. An agent cannot be clothed with greater power than his principal. But, as Congress is bound to protect every citizen in his rights of property wherever Congress has jurisdiction, it follows that Congress is bound to protect the slaveholder, who settles in the Territories with his slaves, in the full enjoyment of that species of property. The slaveholder justly claims protection in the Territories by reason of the fact that his State is a co-equal sovereign in the ownership; and as long as the domain remains in a Territorial condition the settler has the right to demand that the laws be made to protect his property, and that none be enacted to impair or destroy his right. Under this view, each section has a fair and equal chance in the settlement of the public domain; and when the time arrives for the settlers to frame a State Constitution and to assume the mantle of State sovereignty, each section will have had a fair and equal opportunity of being heard in the settlement of the question whether or not the institution of slavery shall be incorporated into the State Constitution.

The question may be asked, however, if this sectional majority does not respect this State Rights doctrine, but rather overrules it, and acts upon the reverse principle, what can you do? The answer is, that as the government will then have become centralized and no longer subserves the end for which it was created, withdraw from it! In its original formation, two kinds of rights were considered of by the States: First, the rights they granted the government; second, the rights they reserved. Hence, there has been inserted in the Constitution an amendment, declaring that the powers which have not been delegated to the United States, nor prohibited to the States, are reserved by the States respectively or to the people. Upon the doctrines of the State Rights school, there has been very little diversity of opinion at the South. They are the only

doctrines that can check a licentious majority from the exercise of all
its selfish ends; the only doctrines upon which a sectional minority can
maintain its rights in the Union.

B.

FIRE-EATERS SEEK TO SPLIT
THE DEMOCRATIC PARTY

❰The Democracy, battered and torn by internal strife, moved
toward the nominating convention of 1860 with uncertainty. Newspapers
and politicians warned that southern extremists would attempt to divide
the Democratic party to assure the election of a Republican and thus
precipitate a new reason for immediate disunion. The Charleston convention deadlocked, depriving Stephen A. Douglas of the necessary two-
thirds majority. The party later met in Baltimore and nominated Douglas, but the southern bolters nominated John C. Breckinridge. Both
during and after the campaign, Douglas was convinced that a conspiracy
had divided the Democracy in order to destroy the Union.

"*A pretext for the clamor of dissolution.*"   Henry A. Wise, governor
of Virginia, writing in 1858, warned a Philadelphia acquaintance that a
faction wished to break up the Democracy in 1860. (John G. Nicolay
and John Hay, *Abraham Lincoln, A History* [New York, 1890], II,
302, n.)]

THE TRUTH is that there is in the South an organized, active, and
dangerous faction, embracing most of the Federal politicians, who are
bent upon bringing about causes of a dissolution of the Union. They
desire a united South, but not a united country. Their hope of embody-
ing a sectional antagonism is to secure a sectional defeat. At heart, they
do not wish the Democracy to be any longer national, united, or
successful. In the name of Democracy they propose to make a nomination for 1860, at Charleston; but an ultra nomination of an extremist on
the slavery issue alone, to unite the South on that one idea, and on that
to have it defeated by a line of sectionalism which will inevitably draw
swords between fanatics on the other. Bear it in mind, then, that they
desire to control a nomination for no other purpose than to have it
defeated by a line of sections. They desire defeat, for no other end than
to make a pretext for the clamor of dissolution. . . .

Yours truly,

Henry A. Wise

[*Mississippi Democrats are working for disunion.*   The Vicksburg
Whig on January 10, 1860, charged that the Mississippi Democratic
party was filled with "fire-eaters" seeking to destroy the Union. (Percy
Lee Rainwater, *Mississippi, Storm Center of Secession, 1856–1861* [Baton
Rouge, La.: Claitor's Book Store, 1938], pp. 90–91.)]

THE MEMBERS of the party are of two sorts. First, fiery, impulsive, chivalrous Southrons who are always angry, always excited—full of "sound and fury"—and who consider themselves as the peculiar guardians of both the honor and the interests of the South. This wing of the "Salamanders" is always placing public affairs in a "crisis"; always sounding alarm notes on the bugle; vociferating evermore, the stale cry, "the Union is in danger"; and with coats off and with sleeves rolled up and clenched fists presented, are ready at all times, (so far as words are concerned and gestures prove anything) for a regular "set to" with an imaginary army of Abolition invaders.

Secondly, we have another type of fire-eaters, altogether different from those sketched viz: Your cold, calculating, frigid, selfish disunionists, per se, who have deliberately calculated the value of the Union: who, under the guise of devotion to the South, are constantly plotting and scheming the dissolution of the Union; who secretly fostering in their hearts high dreams of personal preferment and individual glory, when the Union of the States shall have been broken, and a grand Southern Confederacy constructed out of the fragments; and who, (whilst in dolorous accents of simulated patriotism they profess to deplore the stern necessity which impels them,) are rejoicing with exceeding great joy, over every event which indicates that our national institutions are about to crumble and decay. Incongruous as are the elements of the fire-eaters, they are a unit in the work of disunion. Actuated by dissimilar impulses, and governed by different arguments and motives, the whole party nevertheless agree that the Union must be dissolved; that the Union cannot endure; and that every consideration of patriotism demands that we should sever the silken ties which bind us as a great and consolidated nation of freemen.

[*Stephen A. Douglas indicts "an enormous conspiracy."* On May 1, 1861, Douglas, speaking in Chicago a month before his death, charged that a conspiracy had wrecked the Union. (Edward McPherson, *The Political History of the United States of America during the Great Rebellion* [Washington, D.C., 1882], p. 392.)]

THE ELECTION of Mr. Lincoln is a mere pretext. The present secession movement is the result of an enormous conspiracy formed more than a year since—formed by leaders in the Southern Confederacy more than twelve months ago. They use the slavery question as a means to aid the accomplishment of their ends. They desired the election of a northern candidate by a sectional vote, in order to show that the two sections cannot live together. When the history of the two years from the Lecompton question down to the Presidential election shall be written, it will be shown that the scheme was deliberately made to break up this Union.

They desired a northern Republican to be elected by a purely northern vote, and then assign this fact as a reason why the sections cannot live together. If the disunion candidate in the late Presidential contest had carried the united South, their scheme was, the northern candidate successful, to seize the Capital last spring, and by a united South and divided North, hold it. Their scheme was defeated, in the defeat of the disunion candidates in several of the southern States.

But this is no time for a detail of causes. The conspiracy is now known; armies have been raised, war is levied to accomplish it. There are only two sides to the question. Every man must be for the United States or against it. There can be no neutrals in this war; *only patriots or traitors!* (Cheer after cheer.)

LINCOLN'S ELECTION PRECIPITATES

THE CRISIS

By October, 1860, most political observers believed that Abraham Lincoln would carry the election. State elections in Indiana and Pennsylvania indicated a strong current favoring the Republican party, and secession talk in southern states increased correspondingly. A full month before the presidential election, state governors and newspaper editors were surveying the probabilities of disunion. On November 6, Lincoln carried every northern state, save New Jersey, and won 180 electoral votes, or 57 more than the votes of his three opponents combined. Excitement in the southern states grew rapidly. Editorial writers echoed the secessionist calls for bold, prompt action and whipped up popular anxiety. Late in November, the Mississippi legislature formally declared that "the secession of each aggrieved State is the proper remedy." What reasons did the southern spokesmen give for prompt secession? Why were they reluctant to wait for Lincoln to take office before deciding their course of action? What advantages did they see in separate state action? In cooperative action?

A.

GOVERNOR BROWN OF GEORGIA ASKS FOR ARMS

❧On the day after the election, Governor Joseph E. Brown of Georgia sent a special message to his legislature, recommending military preparedness. Nine days later he signed a bill appropriating one million dollars for a military fund "for the protection of the rights and preservation of the liberties of the people of Georgia . . . to be expended by the Governor in such manner as he may deem best for the purpose of placing the State in a condition of defence." (Herbert Fielder, *A Sketch of the Life and Times and Speeches of Joseph E. Brown* [Springfield, Mass., 1883], pp. 168–69.)]

If it is ascertained that the Black Republicans have triumphed over

[22]

us, I recommend the call of a Convention of the people of the State at an early day; and I will cordially unite with the General Assembly in any action, which, in their judgment, may be necessary to the protection of the rights and the preservation of the liberties of the people of Georgia against the further aggressions of an enemy, which, when flushed with victory, will be insolent in the hour of triumph.

For the purpose of putting this State in a defensive condition as fast as possible, and preparing for an emergency which must be met sooner or later, I recommend that the sum of one million dollars be immediately appropriated as a military fund for the ensuing year; and that prompt provision be made for raising such portion of the money as may not be in Treasury as fast as the public necessities may require its expenditure. "Millions for defence, but not a cent for tribute," should be the future motto of the Southern States.

To every demand for further concession, or compromise of our rights, we should reply, "The argument is exhausted," and we now "stand by our arms."

B.

SEPARATE STATE ACTION OR COOPERATIVE ACTION?

❡Very quickly the debate over secession centered on two choices of action: independent secession or cooperative and simultaneous secession. On the day after the election, William L. Yancey pleaded with Alabama leaders to take independent action immediately, for he feared efforts at cooperation with other cotton states would delay or perhaps destroy the opportunity to secede. Judge Amos R. Johnson of Mississippi argued that secession was revolution and that it was paramount to enlist the cooperation of all the slaveholding states. (DuBose, *Life and Times of William Lowndes Yancey*, II, 539–40; Rainwater, *Mississippi, Storm Center of Secession*, pp. 166–67.)]

Yancey: "Let us act for ourselves"

. . . IN THE contingency that consultation shall not produce concert, what then? Shall we, too, like the delaying States, linger in the portals of the government? Shall we remain and all be slaves? Shall we wait to bear our share of the common dishonor? God forbid! (Tremendous applause.) Let us act for ourselves. I have good reason to believe the action of any State will be peaceable, will not be resisted under the present or any probable future administration of public affairs. I believe there will not be power to direct a gun against a sovereign State. Certainly there will be no will to do so during the present administration. If the action of the State be resisted, bloodshed will appeal to blood throbbing in Southern hearts. Our brethren from every Southern State will flock to defend a sister State threatened by mercenary bayonets. To do one's duty is the highest aim in life:

'Tis not the whole of life to live,
Nor all of death to die.

(Tremendous applause.)

Better far to close our days by an act of duty, life's aims fulfilled, than to prolong them through the years weighed down with corroding remembrance that we tamely yielded to our love of ease, or our unworthy fears, that noble heritage which was transmitted to us through toil, sufferings, battle, victory, to go down, unimpaired, to our posterity. As for myself, rather than live on subject to a government which breaks the compact at will and places me in a position of inequality, of inferiority to the Northern free negro, though that life be illustrated with gilded chains by luxury and ease, I would in the cause of my State gather around me some brave spirits who, however few in number, would find a grave which the world would recognize, my countrymen, as a modern Thermopylae. (Vehement and prolonged applause.)

Johnson: "Deliberate Co-operation"

I deprecate . . . all separate State action. The idea of precipitating the cotton States into a revolution, leaving their sisters of other slaveholding States in the Union, not even consulted as to the final movement involving the interest of all, is not for a single moment to be entertained. Co-operation—calm, deliberate co-operation—of the whole section, is the only course we can pursue for a proper adjustment of our affairs. . . .

Separate secession, State by State, and some of the slaveholding States maintaining their position in the Union, would inevitably lead to civil war and carnage. If we act on the principle of co-operation, and are finally forced to revolutionize the government, we shall go out of the Confederacy as a unit, with sufficient physical strength and moral force to maintain ourselves. By co-operation, in the mode indicated, we may secure a bloodless revolution, should we, unfortunately, be driven to that last resort belonging to oppressed humanity.

C.

SOUTHERN EDITORS SPEAK PLAINLY:
DELAY IS DANGEROUS

⟨Newspapers helped to stir up popular excitement and shape the course of action in the cotton states. (Dwight L. Dumond, ed., *Southern Editorials on Secession* [New York: Appleton-Century, Inc., 1931], pp. 204–6; Rainwater, *Mississippi, Storm Center of Secession*, pp. 163–64.)]

Charleston Mercury, *November 3, 1860*

THE ISSUE before the country is the extinction of slavery. No man of common sense, who has observed the progress of events, and who is not prepared to surrender the institution, with the safety and independence of the South, can doubt that the time for action has come—now or never. The Southern States are now in the crisis of their fate; and, if we read aright the signs of the times, nothing is needed for our deliverance, but that the ball of revolution be set in motion. There is sufficient readiness among the people to make it entirely successful. Co-operation will follow the action of any State. The example of a forward movement only is requisite to unite Southern States in a common cause. . . .

The existence of slavery is at stake. The evils of submission are too terrible for us to risk them, from vague fears of failure, or a jealous distrust of our sister Cotton States. We think, therefore, that the approaching Legislature should provide for the assembling of a Convention of the people of South Carolina, as soon as it is ascertained that Messrs. LINCOLN and HAMLIN will have a majority in the Electoral Colleges for President and Vice President of the United States. The only point of difficulty is as *to the time when the Convention shall assemble.* In our judgment, it should assemble *at the earliest possible time* consistent with the opportunity for co-operative action of other Southern States, which may, like ourselves, be determined not to submit to Black Republican domination at Washington. Delay is fatal, while our move will retard no willing State from co-operation. South Carolina, as a sovereign State, is bound to protect her people, but she should so act as to give the other Southern States the opportunity of joining in this policy. The Governors of Alabama, Mississippi and Georgia can act simultaneously. With this qualification, the *earliest time is the best,* for the following reasons:

1. Our great agricultural staples are going to market. The sooner we act, the more of these staples we will have on hand, to control the conduct of the people of the North and of foreign nations, to secure a peaceful result for our deliverance. Thousands at the North, and millions in Europe, need our Cotton to keep their looms in operation. Let us act, before we have parted with our agricultural productions for the season.

2. The commercial and financial interests of the South require that we should act speedily in settling our relations towards the North. Suspense is embarrassment and loss. Decision, with separation, will speedily open new sources of wealth and prosperity, and relieve the finances of the South through the establishment of new channels. . . .

3. The moral effect of promptitude will be immense. Delay will dispirit our friends, and inspire confidence in our enemies. The evils against which we are to provide are not the growth of yesterday. They have been gathering head for thirty years. We have tried, again and again, to avert them by compromise and submission. Submission has failed to avert them; and wise, prompt and resolute action is our last and only course of safety.

4. Black Republican rule at Washington will not commence until the 4th of March next—four short months. Before that time all that South Carolina or the other Southern States intend to do, should be done. The settlement of our relations towards the General Government, in consequence of our measures of protection, should be completed during the existing Administration.

5. It is exceedingly important, also, that our measures should be

laid as soon as possible before *the present Congress*. The secession of one or more States from the Union must be communicated to the President of the United States. He has done all he could do to arrest the sectional madness of the North. He knows that we are wronged and endangered by Black Republican ascendancy, and he will not, we have a right to suppose, lend himself to carry out their bloody policy.

6. By communication from the President of the United States, as well as by the withdrawal from Congress of the members of the seceding States, the question of the right of a State to secede from the Union, with the question of a Force Bill, must arise in Congress for action. The Representatives from the other Southern States will most probably be forced either to continue members of a body which orders the sword to be drawn against the seceding States, or they must leave it. They will most probably leave it; and thus the South will be brought together by action in Congress. . . .

Vicksburg Sun, *November 12, 1860*

It is no time to be timid and over-cautious from a dread of danger. When the enemy is thundering at our gates, it is no time to be taking council of our fears—a blow struck at the right time may turn the whole current in our favor, and place us beyond the reach of storms of disaster and ruin. The South has now the power. Cotton is king—it has always been a great peace-maker, and it is all-powerful to save. The gold and the silver of Europe will come to buy the mimic snow of the South—cotton; and the ships of Europe will come to carry it away, even though Lincoln be President and the South a separate nationality. Safely entrenched behind her cotton bags, she can defy the world—with such a breastwork she can laugh a siege to scorn. Keep out abolition emissaries and we are a match for all the civilized world —for the civilized world depends on the cotton of the South. In case of secession, we shall have more than half the crop on hand, and all the world clamoring for it. Again we say we are independent of the world and can take care of ourselves.

Jackson Mississippian, *November 14, 1860*

Let the final act of secession be taken and fully consummated while the Federal Government is in friendly hands. Much may be accomplished before the 4th of March next. But then we are told that it will be several years before Lincoln will have control of the sword and the purse through the instrumentality of Congress. This furnishes additional argument for action NOW. Let us rally to the protection of our sovereignty, before the enemy can make good his promise to overwhelm us. The issue is upon us. Delay is dangerous. Now is the time to strike. Let not a moment be lost.

IV

SOUTHERN EFFORTS TO FORESTALL

DISUNION FAIL

WITHIN A FEW WEEKS AFTER LINCOLN'S ELECTION THE COTTON STATES were moving rapidly toward secession. Advocates of secession met little opposition from Union men, and most of the discussion turned on the question of expediency and timing, rather than on the theoretical basis of secession as either the right of revolution or the right of a sovereign state. Even those who pleaded the Union cause frequently conceded the principle of secession in theory and, logically, agreed to follow their states whatever the decision. Baffled by the outpouring of secessionist feeling, moderates could only counsel delay, urge concurrent action with other states, and depict the disasters that could befall their states and the whole country. On what grounds did the cooperationists oppose secession? Did they fear or trust Lincoln? Were they unalterably opposed to a southern confederacy?

A.

THE COOPERATIONIST ARGUMENT

❡Percy Lee Rainwater has summarized the cooperationist viewpoints in *Mississippi, Storm Center of Secession*, pp. 183–86.]

NOT ONLY was secession, according to the Co-operationists, a cowardly policy which abandoned without a fight many and valuable vested rights of the South in the Union, but its consummation and the formation of a "Cotton Republic" composed of the Gulf or planting states would be the grossest injustice to the border states and would ultimately bring about the extinction of slavery itself. In the border states the evils of Abolition, it was pointed out, were realities; whereas in the cotton states they were mere abstractions. The more reasonable policy, therefore, was for the border states, if intolerably aggrieved, to initiate aggressive movements and appeal to the cotton states for endorsement and assistance. To such an appeal "real chivalry" would respond with strong arms and hearts. Only a "fictitious chivalry," rash without discretion and courageous only in words, could propose to reverse the plan and set themselves up as judges as to what, and how much, their co-equals should suffer before resorting to revolution. . . . The secession of the cotton states, it was argued, constituted a "base and cowardly desertion" of the northern tier of slave states which had, with the planting states, a common interest in the institution of slavery. Every dictate of honor and justice, therefore, demanded that the border states should not be abandoned until they had, at least, been consulted and had refused to co-operate and agree upon a plan of resistance for the protection of the common interests of all the slaveholding states.

But the dictates of policy and self-interest likewise demanded that the northern and southern tiers of slave states should co-operate for the protection of the institution of slavery. For the cotton states to act independent of, or to desert the border states, would "divide the friends of slavery"; finally abolitionize the deserted states; confine slavery to a very restricted region; and leave it, as Seward desired, "to sting itself to death." The formation of a "Cotton Republic," since the number of slave states in the United States would be thereby diminished, would lead to the constitutional abolition of slavery in the deserted slave states. If abolition were not thus accomplished, the same objective could be speedily effected by slave-stealing on the northern border and slave-selling on the southern border or by the emigration of slaveowners who could or would not sell their slaves. In any event, the slave border would recede gradually southward even to the very borders of Mississippi. The "Cotton Republic," even if able to maintain itself—and that was denied by the Co-operationists—would be too weak to conquer territory to the southward into which slavery might expand. Slavery would thus be confined and hemmed into fixed limits where natural increase of slaves would soon effect the object sought by such men as Greeley and Seward. Caught between the two millstones of inability to expand and the natural increase of its slaves, the boasted "Cotton Republic" would find its slave labor "comparatively worthless."

Furthermore, said the Co-operationist, the secession of the individual planting states and the formation of a "Cotton Republic" could not be achieved without civil war and revolution—"the most prolonged, extensive, and horrible ever recorded in Time's bloody volume." The people should not permit themselves to be deceived by any such "hypocritical nonsense and misnomers as peaceable secession." They should not be deceived by any such "false calculations" or "intoxicated by any such foolish hopes." The only possibility, ran the Co-operation argument, for a bloodless revolution lay in the united and concerted withdrawal of all the slaveholding states from the Federal Union. Such a united South might be strong enough to "insure a peaceable result" and force a "fair division of the territories, the navy and the public property." Such action would, however, be revolution pure and simple and was not justified by existing conditions. . . .

What, then, did the Co-operationists propose as a remedy for the existing evil? In the first place, the Co-operationists proposed to employ all the remedies which the form of the Constitution afforded to check-mate Lincoln in the attempted pursuance of any other course than a purely national one. The legitimate checks of the Constitution were pointed out as being entirely adequate, for the present, to enable the slaveholding states to keep a "full and perfect control of the sectional madness of the day" and to bring about, if necessary, a complete stalemate in the government. "These checks," said Josiah Winchester, "are remedies within the Union, and under the Constitution." "Let the government pause, but not be destroyed; let its function be suspended, but not extinguished; let the flame grow dim, but not be altogether quenched!" The remedies thus prepared by the Founding Fathers for just such an emergency would, it was believed, be quite sufficient to compel Lincoln to abandon, at least temporarily, the sectional position of his party. In the meantime, argued the Co-operationists,

> a convention of all the States can be called; not a sectional but a national body. There the rightful demands of the South can be presented; there the fifteen states can tell their eighteen sisters that under the Constitution the latter have no rights to combine, and will not be allowed to combine, against them; that the combination, while it lasts, will be resisted, within the Union and under the Constitution, by every means the latter allows. They can tell them that it is not the man, Lincoln, they fear, but the principle, combination to aggress, which they resist; that government must and shall stop unless the President acts nationally; that if that combination goes further, and obtains possession of the legislative department as well as the executive, then, the present Constitution having proved inefficient to protect the principle of equality among the States, new guarantees must be yielded by the North, or the compact of Union must be dissolved by joint consent.

If the free states continued to combine as a section against the South and refused either to give new guarantees for the further and adequate protection of the slaveholding states or, having refused further guarantees, to consent to a dissolution of the Union upon terms of an equitable division of the public property, then the Co-operationists were for plunging into the "angry waters of revolution." In such an eventuality the slaveholding states would be united and might reasonably expect to succeed in founding and maintaining an independent Southern Republic. But viewed, even in this favorable light, disunion was little more than cutting off "our nose to spite our face" or of committing "suicide for fear we shall die a natural death."

B.

A SOUTH CAROLINIAN PLEADS FOR THE UNION

⁋Benjamin F. Perry, one-time foe of nullification, also fought secession. He attacked the folly of disunion in a long public letter reprinted in part below and dated August 13, 1860. But a few months later when his state voted to secede, Perry exclaimed, "You are all now going to the devil and I will go with you. Honor and patriotism require me to stand by my State." He accepted offices under the Confederate government. (B. F. Perry, *Biographical Sketches of Eminent American Statesmen, with Speeches, Addresses and Letters by Ex-Governor B. F. Perry, of Greenville, S.C.* [Philadelphia, 1887], pp. 171–80.)]

Is THE election of a Chief Magistrate of the Republic sufficient cause for the destruction of the Federal Government and all the horrors of civil war and revolution? This is a grave and momentous question, and should be calmly and dispassionately considered in all its bearings before it is answered by the patriot and statesman. They who consider the union of the States an injury and a curse to the South, and are disunionists *per se*, will, of course, answer promptly in the affirmative. Their minds are already made up, and their purpose formed. To them it is a matter of no consequence how an event so desirable is brought about.

But there are others who think differently of the Federal Union. They have seen this American Republic, the only free government in the world, prosper and flourish as no government ever did in ancient or modern times. In the course of seventy or eighty years we have increased from thirteen States to thirty-three States, from three millions of people to thirty millions, from poverty and weakness to wealth, power and grandeur, unsurpassed by the oldest and greatest nations of the earth. A wilderness, covering a vast continent, has been converted into towns, cities and cultivated fields. During all this time every one has enjoyed the most perfect freedom and security in all his rights as a citizen. At home and abroad we have commanded the respect and admiration of the world. In the remotest corners of the earth an American citizen knows and feels that he has a government able and willing to protect him, and that no power on earth dare molest him.

It is natural that they who thus reflect, and remember the farewell advice of the Father of His Country, *that union and liberty are insepa-rable*, who know from history, in all ages, the horrors of civil war, and the dangers of revolution to liberty and civil government, should wish and earnestly desire the perpetuity of the Republic, under which they live so happily. With such one may well reason and argue without giving offence, and ask for a calm and dispassionate determination before they decide on breaking up their Government, and running the hazard of forming a better one.

The probability is that the Black Republican candidate will be elected President of the United States. It is a grievous misfortune, and one to be deeply lamented by every citizen of the South. But it must be remembered that the Southern States will have brought this misfortune, grievous as it may be, on themselves, by their own divisions and party strifes. Nothing can be more clearly shown. It was predicted at the time, and the South forewarned of the impending danger. . . .

Lincoln will be elected President in consequence of [the] disruption of the Democratic party. He will be elected by *one-third* of the voters of the United States! . . . Lincoln will come into power with two-thirds of the people of the United States opposed to his administration! This ought, in some measure, to appease the apprehensions of those who affect to be so much alarmed for the South. His administration will commence a weak one, and it is not probable that he can, backed by one-third of the people of the United States, seriously injure and oppress the other two-thirds.

But we have another check on his ability to do mischief. A majority of the Senate of the United States will be opposed to his administration, and no bill can become a law till it receives the sanction of the Senate. This majority in the Senate cannot be changed for several years to come. It is doubtful, too, as to the majority of the House of Representatives. More than likely the next election will give a majority of the members of the House in opposition to the Black Republicans. This is to be inferred from the popular vote of two-thirds against Lincoln in the Presidential election. . . .

Judging from the course pursued by other Presidents, and that policy which usually governs politicians whilst in power, instead of doing any rash, violent or unconstitutional act to injure or offend those opposed to him, it is likely Lincoln will pursue a very cautious, politic and wise course towards the South. It cannot be in the nature of any man elevated to the Presidency to wish to see the Government broken up under his Administration, the Republic dismembered, and the country plunged into a civil war. Very likely his great effort will be to acquire popularity in the Southern States, and appease their opposition by a rigid adherence to the Constitution and respect for the rights of the South. It is not at all improbable that the South may find more favors under the Administration of Lincoln than they have under any Democratic Administration. It may be that "Old Abe" will go out of office quite a favorite with the Southern people! At least we should give him a trial.

The election of President, in conformity with the Federal Constitution, is no ground whatever for breaking up the Republic, no matter how bitterly opposed to him we may be. We must wait and decide on his acts and measures; nothing less will justify us in the eyes of the world, or in the opinions of our people. To inculcate the notion that a portion of the citizens of a Republic may break up and revolutionize their Government, because they have been defeated in their choice of a Chief Magistrate, is the repudiation of the first principles of republicanism, and sanctioning that which leads inevitably to lawless despotism. . . .

It may be that I am mistaken in supposing slavery to be out of the reach of the assaults of its foes, and if so I will be as ready as any one to defend it at the sacrifice of the Union itself, as much as I value the Union. But I am not willing to act prematurely when there is no danger. As to dissolving the Union on a mere abstraction, the right to carry slaves where slave-holders never desire to carry them, and where they would be worthless if carried, I am opposed to it now and forever; and shall endeavor to defend the rights of the South in the Union, where I think they have been heretofore properly defended, and may still be defended if the South is true to herself and united in that defence.

That all who were Disunionists should have rejoiced at the breaking up of the Democratic Convention in Charleston is very natural. They saw in that movement the destruction of the National Democracy and their defeat in the coming Presidential election. They saw in the future the election of a Black Republican, and knew what a powerful lever it would be in their hands to wield against the Union. But that any friend to the Federal Union and lover of the peace and quiet of the Republic should have rejoiced at such a dire calamity, is most amazing. The Democratic party had been the friends of the South and the rights of the States, the true supporters and defenders of the Constitution, and the only just and wise rulers of the Government from its foundation to the present time. Under their administration the boundaries of the Republic had been enlarged by the acquisition of Louisiana, Florida, Texas, California and Oregon. The rights and honor of the Republic had been gallantly defended in a war with Great Britain and with Mexico. How any patriot could chuckle and grin over the death of this glorious old party is more than I can comprehend.

But it does seem that for years past there has been at the South a systematic organization to weaken and drive from the Democratic party all who stand by it and fight for it in the Northern States. Their aim is to sectionalize parties, as the Black Republicans have done at the North! as the Federalists did during the war of 1812! all of which Washington denounced as fatal to the Republic, fatal to our Independence, and fatal to Liberty itself.

Disunion—a word of horrible import to the illustrious sages of the Republic, one which was not to be breathed by Washington, Jefferson, Madison, Monroe, and Jackson—is now in the mouth of every flippant politician, certain newspaper editor, half-educated schoolboy, and unthinking mortal. It is the high road to office and popularity, and he who dare repeat the dying bequest of the Father of His Country is branded a traitor. The same feeling is manifested in the Northern States by the Black Republicans and John Brown sympathizers. Well may it be said, we have fallen on evil times; and that "those whom the gods intend to destroy, they first make mad."

To consummate this folly it is proposed for South Carolina to march out of the Union solitary and alone. That if left alone we shall do very well, and if an attempt is made to force us back, the South will rally to the rescue. We had better not depend on being let alone if we oppose the collection of duties. We may withdraw our members of Congress and no one will disturb us. In 1851 President Fillmore did not manifest any disposition to let us alone. He sent troops to Charleston. Gen. Jackson did the same in 1831. We must not, therefore, expect to be let alone. Will the other Southern States rally to our assistance in doing that which they themselves think it advisable not to do? Would it not be more prudent to get them to unite with us beforehand? And if they will not unite in our action, for us to stay with them till some act is done which will unite the South?

There is no doubt at all if the whole South were united in any course, they could take care of themselves in any emergency. The proper course for South Carolina to pursue is to say to the other Southern States she is ready to act with them, and to await their action, whatever that may be. This will prevent her playing before high Heaven a ridiculous farce or a bloody tragedy.

C.

WAS SECESSION POPULAR?

❡Two newspaper accounts give different views of the popular attitude toward secession. Both were published in the same week. (Moore, *The Rebellion Record*, I, "Diary," 12, 20.)]

Atlanta Southern Confederacy, *January 8, 1861*

IT IS a notable fact, that, wherever the "Minute Men," as they are called, have had an organization, those counties have voted, by large majorities, for immediate secession. Those that they could not control by persuasion and coaxing, *they dragooned and bullied, by threats, jeers, and sneers.* By this means thousands of good citizens were induced to vote the immediate secession ticket through timidity. Besides, the towns and citizens have been flooded with sensation dispatches and inflammatory rumors, manufactured in Washington city for the especial occasion. To be candid, there never has been as much lying and bullying practised, in the same length of time, since the destruction of Sodom and Gomorrah, as has been in the recent State campaign. The fault has been at Washington city; from that cess-pool have emanated all the abominations that ever cursed a free people.

Mobile Advertiser, *January 12, 1861*

Yesterday was the wildest day of excitement in the annals of Mobile. The whole people seemed to be at the top point of enthusiasm from the time the telegraphic announcement of the passage of the secession ordinance in the convention was received, until the hour when honest men should be abed. To add, if possible, to the excitement, the news of the secession of our sister State of Florida was received simultaneously with that of the withdrawal of Alabama.

Immediately on the receipt of the news, an immense crowd assembled at the "secession pole," at the foot of Government-street, to witness the spreading of the Southern flag, and it was run up amid the shouts of the multitude and the thunders of cannon. One hundred and one guns for Alabama and fifteen for Florida were fired. . . .

The military paraded the streets. The Cadets were out in force, bearing the splendid flag which was presented them the day previous, and is a most gorgeous banner, and, with the Independent Rifles, marched to Bienville Square, where they fired continuous salvos of musketry.

The demonstration at night was worthy the magnitude of the event celebrated. The display was of the most brilliant description. . . . When night fell, the city emerged from darkness into a blaze of such glory as could only be achieved by the most recklessly extravagant consumption of tar and tallow. The broad boulevard of Government-street was an avenue of light, bonfires of tar-barrels being kindled at intervals of a square's distance along its length, and many residences upon it were illuminated. The Court House and other buildings at the intersection of Royal-street shone with a plenitude of candles. . . .

In the remote, unfrequented streets of the city, as well as in the more prominent avenues of business or residence, frequent illuminated buildings could be seen dispersing the gloom of night from about them. Rockets blazed and crackers popped, and the people hurrahed and shouted as they never did before. The streets, as light as day, were overflowed with crowds of ladies who had turned out to see the display. Many of the designs of illuminatory work were exceedingly tasteful and beautiful. The "Southern Cross" was a favored emblematic pattern, and gleaming in lines of fire, competed with the oft-repeated "Lone Star" for admiration and applause from the multitude. In short, the occasion seemed several Fourth of Julys, a number of New Year's eves, various Christmases, and a sprinkling of other holidays all rolled into one big event. . . .

V

BUCHANAN'S DILEMMA

PRESIDENT JAMES BUCHANAN HOPED THE SECESSION STORM WOULD NOT break until he left office on March 4, 1861, but his seemingly weak and confused response to the crisis probably emboldened the disunionists. In contrast with President Jackson's vigorous response to the nullification crisis, Buchanan publicly declared on December 3, 1860, that he saw just cause for the South's irritation and that he could do nothing within the existing laws to thwart secession by force, even though he did not recognize secession as being constitutional. Instead, Buchanan recommended conciliation via an "explanatory" constitutional amendment protecting slavery. Meanwhile, high officials within Buchanan's administration were privately urging their states to secede, preferably after Lincoln's inauguration, and were helping southern governors buy surplus arms from federal arsenals. Confident that the President would not use force to prevent the seizure of federal forts, mints, and customs houses, South Carolina hastened to secede, much to Buchanan's discomfort. While the President wrung his hands, besought constitutional and legal remedies, and tried to reassure the cotton states that his administration intended no show of force, more states departed from the Union. In the seceding states, federal judges, customs collectors, and marshals resigned their posts, leaving the President without officials to carry out the laws.

Why did President Buchanan refuse to ask for extraordinary powers to put down the secessionists? Under the circumstances, was Buchanan correct in refusing to act swiftly to put down incipient rebellion? Would an "explanatory" amendment have resolved the crisis?

A.

CONSPIRACY GRIPS BUCHANAN'S ADMINISTRATION

⟪After Mr. Buchanan left office, Republicans frequently charged that the President had fallen into the clutches of persuasive secessionists and that the success of the southern states in destroying the Union was in part due to these false advisers. John G. Nicolay, former private secretary to President Lincoln, believed a "cabal" controlled Buchanan during the critical period. (Nicolay, *The Outbreak of Rebellion*, pp. 17–19; Nicolay and Hay, *Abraham Lincoln, A History*, II, 317–19, 325–26.)]

CONSPIRACY WAS not confined to South Carolina or the Cotton States; unfortunately, it had established itself in the highest official circles of the national administration. Three members of President Buchanan's cabinet—[Howell] Cobb of Georgia, Secretary of the Treasury, [John B.] Floyd of Virginia, Secretary of War, and [Jacob] Thompson of Mississippi, Secretary of the Interior—had become ardent and active disunionists. Grouped about these three principal traitors were a number of subordinate and yet influential functionaries, all forming together a central secession cabal, working, in daily and flagrant violation of their official oaths, to promote the success of the Southern conspiracy. After the meeting of Congress, on the first Monday of December, the Senators and Representatives from the Cotton States were in Washington to counsel, prompt, and assist this cabinet cabal, and the President was subjected to the double influence of insidious suggestion from within, and personal pressure from without his administration, acting in regulated concert.

No taint of disloyal purpose or thought appears to attach to President Buchanan; but his condition of mind predisposed him in a remarkable degree to fall under the controlling influence of his disloyal counsellors. He possessed the opposing qualities of feeble will and stubborn prejudice; advancing years and decreasing vigor added to his irresolution and embarrassed his always limited capabilities. In the defeat of Breckinridge, whom he had championed, and in the sweeping success of the Republicans, he had suffered scorching rebuke and deep humiliation. His administration was condemned, his policy was overthrown; his proud party was a hopeless wreck. He had no elasticity of mind, no buoyancy of hope to recover from the shock. Withal he had a blind disbelief in the popular judgment; he refused to recognize the fact of an adverse decision at the ballot-box. After his long affiliation with Southern men in thought and action, he saw, as it were, through Southern eyes; his mind dwelt painfully on the fancied wrongs of the South. His natural impulse, therefore, was to embarrass and thwart the Republican victory by such official utterance and administration as would occur in his brief remainder of office; and this was probably also the first and natural feeling of even the loyal members of his Cabinet, who were prominent and devoted Democratic partisans.

The presidential election decided, it was necessary to begin the preparation of his annual message to Congress, which would convene in less than a month. Just about this time came the thickening reports of Southern insurrection and the ostentatious resignations of the Charleston Federal officials. The first expressions from loyal members of the Cabinet were that rebellion must be put down. But this remedy grated harshly

on Buchanan's prejudices. He had aided these Southern malcontents to
intrigue for slavery, to complain of oppression, to threaten disunion. To
become the public accuser of his late allies and friends, under disaster
and defeat, doubtless seemed desertion and black ingratitude. The Cabinet traitors had no such scruples. They were ready enough to desert
the President, but they wanted first to use him. . . .

Assistant Secretary of State Trescott Conveys Cobb's Views: W. H. Trescott to R. Barnwell Rhett

Washington, Nov. 1, 1860.

Dear Rhett: I received your letter this morning. As to my views or
opinions of the Administration, I can, of course, say nothing. As to Mr.
Cobb's views, he is willing that I should communicate them to you, in
order that they may aid you in forming your own judgment; but, you
will understand that this is confidential—that is, neither Mr. Cobb nor
myself must be quoted as the source of your information. I will not
dwell on this, as you will, on a moment's reflection, see the embarrassment which might be produced by any *authorized* statement of his
opinions. I will only add, by way of preface, that after the very fullest
and freest conversations with him, I feel sure of his earnestness, single-
ness of purpose, and resolution in the whole matter.

Mr. Cobb believes that the time is come for resistance; that upon
the election of Lincoln, Georgia ought to secede from the Union, and
that she will do so; that Georgia and every other State should, as far
as secession, act for herself, resuming her delegated powers, and thus put
herself in position to consult with other sovereign States who take the
same ground. After the secession is effected, then will be the time
to consult. But he is of opinion, most strongly, that whatever action
is resolved on should be consummated on the 4th of March, not
before.

That while the action determined on should be decisive and irrevocable, its initial point should be the 4th of March. He is opposed to
any Southern convention, merely for the purpose of consultation. If a
Southern convention is held, it must be of delegates empowered to act,
whose action is at once binding on the States they represent.

But he desires me to impress upon you his conviction, that any
attempt to precipitate the actual issue upon this Administration will be
most mischievous—calculated to produce differences of opinion and
destroy unanimity. He thinks it of great importance that the cotton
crop should go forward at once, and that the money should be in the
hands of the people, that the cry of popular distress shall not be heard
at the outset of this move.

My own opinion is that it would be well to have a discreet man,
one who knows the value of silence, who can listen wisely, present in
Milledgeville, at the meeting of the [Georgia] State Legislature, as there
will be there an outside gathering of the very ablest men of that State.

And the next point, that you should, at the earliest possible day of
the session of our own [South Carolina] Legislature, elect a man as
governor whose name and character will conciliate as well as give

confidence to all the men of the State,—if we do act, I really think this half the battle,—a man upon whose temper the State can rely.

I say nothing about a convention, as I understand, on all hands, that that is a fixed fact, and I have confined myself to answering your question. I will be much obliged to you if you will write me soon and fully from Columbia.

It is impossible to write to you, with the constant interruption of the office, and as you want Cobb's opinions, not mine, I sent this to you.

Yours,
W. H. T.

Senator Thomas L. Clingman of North Carolina Recalls an Episode

About the middle of December [1860] I had occasion to see the Secretary of the Interior on some official business. On my entering the room, Mr. Thompson said to me, "Clingman, I am glad you have called, for I intended presently to go up to the Senate to see you. I have been appointed a commissioner by the State of Mississippi to go down to North Carolina to get your State to secede, and I wished to talk with you about your Legislature before I start down in the morning to Raleigh, and to learn what you think of my chance of success." I said to him, "I did not know that you had resigned." He answered, "Oh, no, I have not resigned." "Then," I replied, "I suppose you resign in the morning." "No," he answered, "I do not intend to resign, for Mr. Buchanan wished us all to hold on, and go out with him on the 4th of March." "But," said I, "does Mr. Buchanan know for what purpose you are going to North Carolina?" "Certainly," he said, "he knows my object." Being surprised by this statement, I told Mr. Thompson that Mr. Buchanan was probably so much perplexed by his situation that he had not fully considered the matter, and that as he was already involved in difficulty, we ought not to add to his burdens; and then suggested to Mr. Thompson that he had better see Mr. Buchanan again, and by way of inducing him to think the matter over, mention what I had been saying to him. Mr. Thompson said, "Well, I can do so, but I think he fully understands it." In the evening I met Mr. Thompson at a small social party, and as soon as I approached him, he said, "I knew I could not be mistaken. I told Mr. Buchanan all you said, and he told me that he wished me to go, and hoped I might succeed." I could not help exclaiming, "Was there ever before any potentate who sent out his own Cabinet ministers to excite an insurrection against his Government!"

B.

THE PRESIDENT'S STAND ON SECESSION

❡Aware that the cotton states were moving toward secession, President Buchanan, after consultation with his cabinet, set forth his views in his fourth and final annual message to Congress. The message pleased neither North nor South. Senator William Henry Seward, leading Republican spokesman in the Senate, sneered that "the President has conclusively proved two things: (1) That no State has the right to secede unless it wishes to; and (2) that it is the President's duty to enforce the laws unless somebody opposes him." Senator Louis T. Wigfall of Texas declared, "I confess, sir, that I do not understand it; and the more I read it the less do I comprehend it." In the light of subsequent events, John G. Nicolay pronounced it "a specimen of absurdity, stupidity, and wilful wrong-headedness . . . not equalled in American political literature." George Ticknor Curtis, Buchanan's biographer, later defended the President's position on the ground that the alternative to a peaceful solution was military despotism. "It is perfectly plain," Curtis stated in 1883, "that if Buchanan had resorted to any other means than those which the Constitution had provided for, we should have had this constitutional Government converted into a military despotism more than twenty years ago." (James D. Richardson, *A Compilation of the Messages and Papers of the Presidents, 1789–1897* [Washington, 1900], V, 626–39.)]

Fourth Annual Message

Washington City, December 3, 1860.

FELLOW-CITIZENS of the Senate and House of Representatives:

. . . The long-continued and intemperate interference of the Northern people with the question of slavery in the Southern States has at length produced its natural effects. The different sections of the Union are now arrayed against each other, and the time has arrived, so much dreaded by the Father of his Country, when hostile geographical parties have been formed.

I have long foreseen and often forewarned my countrymen of the now impending danger. This does not proceed solely from the claim on the part of Congress or the Territorial legislatures to exclude slavery from the Territories, nor from the efforts of different States to defeat the execution of the fugitive-slave law. All or any of these evils might have been endured by the South without danger to the Union (as others have been) in the hope that time and reflection might apply the remedy. The immediate peril arises not so much from these causes as from the fact that the incessant and violent agitation of the slavery question throughout the North for the last quarter of a century has at length produced its malign influence on the slaves and inspired them with vague notions of freedom. Hence a sense of security no longer exists around the family altar. This feeling of peace at home has given place to apprehensions of servile insurrections. Many a matron throughout the South retires at night in dread of what may befall herself and children before the morning. Should this apprehension of domestic danger, whether real or imaginary, extend and intensify itself until it shall pervade the masses of the Southern people, then disunion will become inevitable. Self-preservation is the first law of nature, and has been implanted in the heart of man by his Creator for the wisest purpose; and no political union, however fraught with blessings and benefits in all other respects, can long continue if the necessary consequence be to render the homes and the firesides of nearly half the parties to it habitually and hopelessly insecure. Sooner or later the bonds of such a union must be severed. It is my conviction that this fatal period has not yet arrived, and my prayer to God is that He would preserve the Constitution and the Union throughout all generations.

But let us take warning in time and remove the cause of danger. It can not be denied that for five and twenty years the agitation at the North against slavery has been incessant. . . . This agitation has ever since been continued by the public press, by the proceedings of State and county conventions and by abolition sermons and lectures. The time of Congress has been occupied in violent speeches on this never-ending subject, and appeals, in pamphlet and other forms, indorsed by distinguished names, have been sent forth from this central point and spread broadcast over the Union.

How easy would it be for the American people to settle the slavery question forever and to restore peace and harmony to this distracted country! They, and they alone, can do it. All that is necessary to accomplish the object, and all for which the slave States have ever contended, is to be let alone and permitted to manage their domestic institutions in their own way. As sovereign States, they, and they alone, are responsible before God and the world for the slavery existing among them. For this the people of the North are not more responsible and have no more right to interfere than with similar institutions in Russia or in Brazil.

Upon their good sense and patriotic forbearance I confess I still greatly rely. Without their aid it is beyond the power of any President, no matter what may be his own political proclivities, to restore peace and harmony among the States. Wisely limited and restrained as is his power under our Constitution and laws, he alone can accomplish but little for good or for evil on such a momentous question.

And this brings me to observe that the election of any one of our fellow-citizens to the office of President does not of itself afford just cause for dissolving the Union. This is more especially true if his election has been effected by a mere plurality, and not a majority of the people, and has resulted from transient and temporary causes, which may probably never again occur. In order to justify a resort to revolutionary resistance, the Federal Government must be guilty of "a deliberate, palpable, and dangerous exercise" of powers not granted by the Constitution. The late Presidential election, however, has been held in strict conformity with its express provisions. How, then, can the result justify a revolution to destroy this very Constitution? Reason, justice, a regard for the Constitution, all require that we shall wait for some overt and dangerous act on the part of the President elect before resorting to such a remedy. It is said, however, that the antecedents of the President elect have been sufficient to justify the fears of the South that he will attempt to invade their constitutional rights. But are such apprehensions of contingent danger in the future sufficient to justify the immediate destruction of the noblest system of government ever devised by mortals? From the very nature of his office and its high responsibilities he must necessarily be conservative. The stern duty of administering the vast and complicated concerns of this Government affords in itself a guaranty that he will not attempt any violation of a clear constitutional right.

After all, he is no more than the chief executive officer of the Government. His province is not to make but to execute the laws. And it is a remarkable fact in our history that, notwithstanding the repeated efforts of the antislavery party, no single act has ever passed Congress, unless we may possibly except the Missouri compromise, impairing in the slightest degree the rights of the South to their property in slaves; and it may also be observed, judging from present indications, that no probability exists of the passage of such an act by a majority of both Houses, either in the present or the next Congress. Surely under these circumstances we ought to be restrained from present action by the precept of Him who spake as man never spoke, that "sufficient unto the day is the evil thereof." The day of evil may never come unless we shall rashly bring it upon ourselves.

It is alleged as one cause for immediate secession that the Southern States are denied equal rights with the other States in the common Territories. But by what authority are these denied? Not by Congress, which has never passed, and I believe never will pass, any act to exclude slavery from these Territories; and certainly not by the Supreme Court, which has solemnly decided that slaves are property, and, like all other property, their owners have a right to take them into the common Territories and hold them there under the protection of the Constitution.

So far, then, as Congress is concerned, the objection is not to anything they have already done, but to what they may do hereafter. It will surely be admitted that this apprehension of future danger is no good reason for an immediate dissolution of the Union. . . .

The most palpable violations of constitutional duty which have been committed consist in the acts of different State legislatures to defeat the execution of the fugitive-slave law. It ought to be remembered, however, that for these acts neither Congress nor any President can justly be held responsible. Having been passed in violation of the Federal Constitution, they are therefore null and void. All the courts, both State and national, before whom the question has arisen have from the beginning declared the fugitive-slave law to be constitutional. The single exception is that of a State court in Wisconsin, and this has not only been reversed by the proper appellate tribunal, but has met with such universal reprobation that there can be no danger from it as a precedent. The validity of this law has been established over and over again by the Supreme Court of the United States with perfect unanimity. It is founded upon an express provision of the Constitution, requiring that fugitive slaves who escape from service in one State to another shall be "delivered up" to their masters. Without this provision it is a well-known historical fact that the Constitution itself could never have been adopted by the Convention. In one form or other, under the acts of 1793 and 1850, both being substantially the same, the fugitive-slave law has been the law of the land from the days of Washington until the present moment. Here, then, a clear case is presented in which it will be the duty of the next President, as it has been my own, to act with vigor in executing this supreme law against the conflicting enactments of State legislatures. Should he fail in the performance of this high duty, he will then have manifested a disregard of the Constitution and laws, to the great injury of the people of nearly one-half of the States of the Union. But are we to presume in advance that he will thus violate his duty? This would be at war with every principle of justice and of Christian charity. Let us wait for the overt act. The fugitive-slave law has been carried into execution in every contested case since the commencement of the present Administration, though often, it is to be regretted, with great loss and inconvenience to the master and with considerable expense to the Government. Let us trust that the State legislatures will repeal their unconstitutional and obnoxious enactments. Unless this shall be done without unnecessary delay, it is impossible for any human power to save the Union.

The Southern States, standing on the basis of the Constitution, have a right to demand this act of justice from the States of the North. Should it be refused, then the Constitution, to which all the States are parties, will have been willfully violated by one portion of them in a provision essential to the domestic security and happiness of the remainder. In that event the injured States, after having first used all peaceful and constitutional means to obtain redress, would be justified in revolutionary resistance to the Government of the Union.

I have purposely confined my remarks to revolutionary resistance, because it has been claimed within the last few years that any State, whenever this shall be its sovereign will and pleasure, may secede from the Union in accordance with the Constitution and without any violation of the constitutional rights of the other members of the Confederacy; that as each became parties to the Union by the vote of its own people assembled in convention, so any one of them may retire from the Union in a similar manner by the vote of such a convention.

In order to justify secession as a constitutional remedy, it must be on the principle that the Federal Government is a mere voluntary association of States, to be dissolved at pleasure by any one of the contracting parties. If this be so, the Confederacy is a rope of sand, to be penetrated and dissolved by the first adverse wave of public opinion in any of the States. In this manner our thirty-three States may resolve themselves into as many petty, jarring, and hostile republics, each one retiring from the Union without responsibility whenever any sudden excitement might impel them to such a course. By this process a Union might be entirely broken into fragments in a few weeks which cost our forefathers many years of toil, privation, and blood to establish.

Such a principle is wholly inconsistent with the history as well as the character of the Federal Constitution. After it was framed with the greatest deliberation and care it was submitted to conventions of the people of the several States for ratification. Its provisions were discussed at length in these bodies, composed of the first men of the country. Its opponents contended that it conferred powers upon the Federal Government dangerous to the rights of the States, whilst its advocates maintained that under a fair construction of the instrument there was no foundation for such apprehensions. In that mighty struggle between the first intellects of this or any other country it never occurred to any individual, either among its opponents or advocates, to assert or even to intimate that their efforts were all vain labor, because the moment that any State felt herself aggrieved she might secede from the Union. What a crushing argument would this have proved against those who dreaded that the rights of the States would be endangered by the Constitution! The truth is that it was not until many years after the origin of the Federal Government that such a proposition was first advanced. It was then met and refuted by the conclusive arguments of General Jackson, who in his message of the 16th of January, 1833, transmitting the nullifying ordinance of South Carolina to Congress, employs the following language:

> The right of the people of a single State to absolve themselves at will and without the consent of the other States from their most solemn obligations, and hazard the liberties and happiness of the millions composing this Union, can not be acknowledged. Such authority is believed to be utterly repugnant both to the principles upon which the General Government is constituted and to the objects which it is expressly formed to attain.

> . . . [The Union] was intended to be perpetual, and not to be annulled at the pleasure of any one of the contracting parties. The old Articles of Confederation were entitled "Articles of Confederation and Perpetual Union between the States," and by the thirteenth article it was expressly declared that "the articles of this Confederation shall be inviolably observed by every State, and the Union shall be perpetual." The preamble to the Constitution of the United States, having express reference to the Articles of Confederation, recites that it was established "in order to form a more perfect union." And yet it is contended that this "more perfect union" does not include the essential attribute of perpetuity.

> But that the Union was designed to be perpetual appears conclusively from the nature and extent of the powers conferred by the Constitution on the Federal Government. These powers embrace the very highest attributes of national sovereignty. They place both the sword and the purse under its control. Congress has power to make war and to make peace, to raise and support armies and navies, and to conclude treaties with foreign governments. It is invested with the power to coin money and to regulate the value thereof, and to regulate commerce with foreign nations and among the several States. It is not necessary to enumerate the other high powers which have been conferred upon the Federal Government. In order to carry the enumerated powers into effect, Congress possesses the exclusive right to lay and collect duties on imports, and, in common with the States, to lay and collect all other taxes. . . .

> This Government, therefore, is a great and powerful Government, invested with all the attributes of sovereignty over the special subjects

to which its authority extends. Its framers never intended to implant in its bosom the seeds of its own destruction, nor were they at its creation guilty of the absurdity of providing for its own dissolution. It was not intended by its framers to be the baseless fabric of a vision, which at the touch of the enchanter would vanish into thin air, but a substantial and mighty fabric, capable of resisting the slow decay of time and of defying the storms of ages. Indeed, well may the jealous patriots of that day have indulged fears that a Government of such high powers might violate the reserved rights of the States, and wisely did they adopt the rule of a strict construction of these powers to prevent the danger. But they did not fear, nor had they any reason to imagine, that the Constitution would ever be so interpreted as to enable any State by her own act, and without the consent of her sister States, to discharge her people from all or any of their federal obligations.

It may be asked, then, Are the people of the States without redress against the tyranny and oppression of the Federal Government? By no means. The right of resistance on the part of the governed against the oppression of their governments can not be denied. It exists independently of all constitutions, and has been exercised at all periods of the world's history. Under it old governments have been destroyed and new ones have taken their place. It is embodied in strong and express language in our own Declaration of Independence. But the distinction must ever be observed that this is revolution against an established government, and not a voluntary secession from it by virtue of an inherent constitutional right. In short, let us look the danger fairly in the face. Secession is neither more nor less than revolution. It may or it may not be a justifiable revolution, but still it is revolution. . . .

Apart from the execution of the laws, so far as this may be practicable, the Executive has no authority to decide what shall be the relations between the Federal Government and South Carolina. He has been invested with no such discretion. He possesses no power to change the relations heretofore existing between them, much less to acknowledge the independence of that State. This would be to invest a mere executive officer with the power of recognizing the dissolution of the confederacy among our thirty-three sovereign States. It bears no resemblance to the recognition of a foreign de facto government, involving no such responsibility. Any attempt to do this would, on his part, be a naked act of usurpation. It is therefore my duty to submit to Congress the whole question in all its bearings. The course of events is so rapidly hastening forward that the emergency may soon arise when you may be called upon to decide the momentous question whether you possess the power by force of arms to compel a State to remain in the Union. I should feel myself recreant to my duty were I not to express an opinion on this important subject.

The question fairly stated is, Has the Constitution delegated to Congress the power to coerce a State into submission which is attempting to withdraw or has actually withdrawn from the Confederacy? If answered in the affirmative, it must be on the principle that the power has been conferred upon Congress to declare and to make war against a State. After much serious reflection I have arrived at the conclusion that no such power has been delegated to Congress or to any other department of the Federal Government. It is manifest upon an inspection of the Constitution that this is not among the specific and enumerated powers granted to Congress, and it is equally apparent that its exercise is not "necessary and proper for carrying into execution" any one of these powers. So far from this power having been delegated to Congress, it was expressly refused by the Convention which framed the Constitution. . . .

Without descending to particulars, it may be safely asserted that the power to make war against a State is at variance with the whole spirit and intent of the Constitution. Suppose such a war should result in the conquest of a State; how are we to govern it afterwards? Shall we hold it as a province and govern it by despotic power? In the nature of things, we could not by physical force control the will of the people and compel them to select Senators and Representatives to Congress and to perform all the other duties depending upon their own volition and required from the free citizens of a free State as a constituent member of the Confederacy.

But if we possessed this power, would it be wise to exercise it under existing circumstances? The object would doubtless be to preserve the Union. War would not only present the most effectual means of destroying it, but would vanquish all hope of its peaceable reconstruction. Besides, in the fraternal conflict a vast amount of blood and treasure would be expended, rendering future reconciliation between the States impossible. In the meantime, who can foretell what would be the sufferings and privations of the people during its existence?

The fact is that our Union rests upon public opinion, and can never be cemented by the blood of its citizens shed in civil war. If it can not live in the affections of the people, it must one day perish. Congress possesses many means of preserving it by conciliation, but the sword was not placed in their hand to preserve it by force.

But may I be permitted solemnly to invoke my countrymen to pause and deliberate before they determine to destroy this grandest temple which has ever been dedicated to human freedom since the world began? It has been consecrated by the blood of our fathers, by the glories of the past, and by the hopes of the future. The Union has already made us the most prosperous, and ere long will, if preserved, render us the most powerful, nation on the face of the earth. In every foreign region of the globe the title of American citizen is held in the highest respect, and when pronounced in a foreign land it causes the hearts of our countrymen to swell with honest pride. Surely when we reach the brink of the yawning abyss we shall recoil with horror from the last fatal plunge.

By such a dread catastrophe the hopes of the friends of freedom throughout the world would be destroyed, and a long night of leaden despotism would enshroud the nations. Our example of more than eighty years would not only be lost, but it would be quoted as a conclusive proof that man is unfit for self-government.

It is not every wrong—nay, it is not every grievous wrong—which can justify a resort to such a fearful alternative. This ought to be the last desperate remedy of a despairing people, after every other constitutional means of conciliation has been exhausted. We should reflect that under this free Government there is an incessant ebb and flow of public opinion. The slavery question, like everything human, will have its day. I firmly believe that it has reached and passed the culminating point. But if in the midst of the existing excitement the Union shall perish, the evil may then become irreparable.

Congress can contribute much to avert it by proposing and recommending to the legislatures of the several States the remedy for existing evils which the Constitution has itself provided for its own preservation. This has been tried at different critical periods of our history, and always with eminent success. . . . I earnestly recommend . . . an "explanatory amendment" of the Constitution on the subject of slavery. This might originate with Congress or the State legislatures, as may be deemed most advisable to attain the object. The explanatory amendment might be confined to the final settlement of the true construction of the Constitution on three special points:

1. An express recognition of the right of property in slaves in the States where it now exists or may hereafter exist.

2. The duty of protecting this right in all the common Territories throughout their Territorial existence, and until they shall be admitted as States into the Union, with or without slavery, as their constitutions may prescribe.

3. A like recognition of the right of the master to have his slave who has escaped from one State to another restored and "delivered up" to him, and of the validity of the fugitive-slave law enacted for this purpose, together with a declaration that all State laws impairing or defeating this right are violations of the Constitution, and are consequently null and void. It may be objected that this construction of the Constitution has already been settled by the Supreme Court of the United States, and what more ought to be required? The answer is that a very large proportion of the people of the United States still contest the correctness of this decision, and never will cease from agitation and admit its binding force until clearly established by the people of the several States in their sovereign character. Such an explanatory amendment would, it is believed, forever terminate the existing dissensions, and restore peace and harmony among the States.

It ought not to be doubted that such an appeal to the arbitrament established by the Constitution itself would be received with favor by all the States of the Confederacy. In any event, it ought to be tried in a spirit of conciliation before any of these States shall separate themselves from the Union. . . .

VI

THE REPUBLICANS' RESPONSE

ABRAHAM LINCOLN, THE MAN ABOUT WHOM THE SECESSION CRISIS SWIRLED, remained quietly at Springfield, Illinois, waiting for inauguration day. A few days after the election, urged to issue a statement reassuring the South of his good intentions, Lincoln asserted, "I could say nothing which I have not already said, and which is in print, and open for the inspection of all. To press a repetition of this upon those who *have* listened, is useless; to press it upon those who have *refused* to listen, and still refuse, would be wanting in self-respect" and would suggest timidity "which would excite the contempt of good men, and encourage bad ones to clamor the more loudly." In mid-January, 1861, Lincoln was still not certain whether the secession movement was genuine or merely an attempt to wring concessions from the new Republican administration. "We have just carried an election on principles fairly stated to the people," he explained to a friend. "Now we are told in advance, the government shall be broken up, unless we surrender to those we have beaten, before we take the offices. In this way they are either attempting to play upon us, or they are in dead earnest. Either way, if we surrender, it is the end of us, and of the government. They will repeat the experiment upon us *ad libitum.*"

Senator William Henry Seward of New York, the Republican party's principal spokesman in Washington, D.C., refused to take the secession movement seriously. He viewed it as an irresponsible gesture by disgruntled politicians and was convinced that, in time, they and their people would recover their senses. In the following selections look for possible answers to these questions: Why did Lincoln rule out concessions? Why did Seward belittle the secession movement? Did the Republican leaders correctly judge the seriousness of the secessionists? What alternatives did the Republicans offer to the secession crisis? Were the Republicans more or less realistic than Buchanan in dealing with the secession states?

[47]

A.

SUBMISSION OF THE NORTH OR WAR

❡Republican Senator John P. Hale of New Hampshire, a renowned foe of slavery, reviewed President Buchanan's message and the implications of the secession crisis in a speech before the United States Senate on December 5, 1860. He summarized his party's view that secession was a threat to obtain Republican concessions. (*The Congressional Globe*, 36th Congress, 2d Session, XXX, p. 9.)]

. . . I WAS in hopes that the President would have looked in the face the crisis in which he says the country is, and that his message would be either one thing or another. But, sir, I have read it somewhat carefully. I listened to it as it was read at the desk; and, if I understand it—and I think I do—it is this: South Carolina has just cause for seceding from the Union; that is the first proposition. The second is, that she has no right to secede. The third is, that we have no right to prevent her from seceding. That is the President's message, substantially. He goes on to represent this as a great and powerful country, and that no State has a right to secede from it; but the power of the country, if I understand the President, consists in what Dickens makes the English constitution to be—a power to do nothing at all.

Now, sir, I think it was incumbent upon the President of the United States to point out definitely and recommend to Congress some rule of action, and to tell us what he recommended us to do. But, in my judgment, he has entirely avoided it. He has failed to look the thing in the face. He has acted like the ostrich, which hides her head, and thereby thinks to escape danger. Sir, the only way to escape danger is to look it in the face. I think the country did expect from the President some exposition of a decided policy; and I confess that, for one, I was rather indifferent as to what that policy was that he recommended; but I hoped that it would be something; that it would be decisive. He has utterly failed in that respect.

I think we may as well look this matter right clearly in the face; and I am not going to be long about doing it. I think that this state of affairs looks to one of two things: it looks to absolute submission, not on the part of our southern friends and the southern States, but of the North, to the abandonment of their position—it looks to a surrender of that popular sentiment which has been uttered through the constituted forms of the ballot-box; or it looks to open war. We need not shut our eyes to the fact. It means war, and it means nothing else; and the State which has put herself in the attitude of secession, so looks upon it. She has asked no counsel, she has considered it as a settled question, and she has armed herself. As I understand the aspect of affairs, it looks to that, and it looks to nothing else except unconditional submission on the part of the majority. I did not read the paper— I do not read many papers—but I understand that there was a remedy suggested in a paper printed, I think, in this city, and it was that the

President and the Vice-President should be inaugurated (that would be a great concession!) and then, being inaugurated, they should quietly resign! Well, sir, I am not entirely certain that that would settle the question. I think that after the President and Vice-President-elect had resigned, there would be as much difficulty in settling who was to take their places as there was in settling it before.

I do not wish, sir, to say a word that shall increase any irritation; that shall add any feeling of bitterness to the state of things which really exists in the country, and I would bear and forbear before I would say any thing which would add to this bitterness; but I tell you, sir, the plain, true way is to look this thing in the face—see where we are. And I avow here—I do not know whether or not I shall be sustained by those who usually act with me—if the issue which is presented is that the constitutional will of the public opinion of this country, expressed through the forms of the Constitution, will not be submitted to, and war is the alternative, let it come in any form or in any shape. The Union is dissolved and it cannot be held together as a Union, if that is the alternative upon which we go into an election. If it is preannounced and determined that the voice of the majority expressed through the regular and constituted forms of the Constitution, will not be submitted to, then, sir, this is not a Union of equals, it is a Union of a dictatorial oligarchy on one side, and a herd of slaves and cowards on the other. That is it, sir; nothing more; nothing less. . . .

B.

NATIONALISM AND PATIENCE WILL MELT SECESSIONISM

❡Two days after South Carolina announced to the world that she was no longer a constituent member of the United States of America, Senator Seward spoke in New York City. He plainly indicated that he believed secession to be a humbug, that national and geographical ties bound the states together, and that the crisis would soon evaporate. (Moore, *The Rebellion Record*, I, "Documents and Narratives," 6–7.)]

. . . AND NOW, fellow-citizens, I will speak one word concerning the anomalous condition of our affairs produced by this disposition of some of the American states to secede from the Union. It has taken, as it ought to have taken, the American people and the world by surprise. Why has it taken them by surprise? Because it is unwise and unnatural. It is wise that all the republican states of this continent should be confederated. It is unwise that any of them should attempt to separate. And yet it ought not to have taken us by surprise. Whoever could have imagined that a machine so complicated, so vast, so new, so untried, as this confederated system of republican states, should be exempt from the common lot of states which have figured in the history of the world? A more complex system of government was never devised—never conceived of among men. How strange it is, how unreasonable it is, that we should be surprised that a pin may drop out of this machinery and that the wheel should drag, or that the gudgeon should be worn until the wheel should cease to play with the regular action! How could we expect to subsist for a period of seventy years exempt from the necessity of repairing our political system of government? Every state in this Union is just like the federal Union—a republic. It has its constitution, and its regular system of action. No state is more than seventy years old, and there is not in any one state of this Union a constitution which is more than twenty-five years old; and so certain has it become that no state can adopt a constitution which will last for more than twenty-five years without being repaired and renewed, that in our own state [New York] the constitution which we adopted twenty years ago contains a provision that next year, without any appeal to the people whatever, a convention shall come together in the state of New York and make a new constitution. Is it strange, then, that this complex system of our government should be found, after a lapse of seventy years, to work a little rough, a little unequal, and that it should require that the engineer should look at the machinery to see where the gudgeon is worn out, and to see that the main wheel is kept in motion? . . .

There is no such thing in the book, no such thing in reason, no such thing in philosophy, and no such thing in nature, as any state existing on the continent of North America outside of the United States of America. I do not believe a word of it; and I do not believe it, for a good many reasons. Some I have already hinted at; and one is, because I do not see any good reason given for it. The best reason I see given for it is, that the people of some of the southern states hate us of the free states very badly, and they say that we hate them, and that all love is lost between us. Well, I do not believe a word of that. On the other hand, I do know for myself and for you, that, bating some little differences of opinion about advantages, and about proscription, and about office, and about freedom, and about slavery and all those which are family difficulties, for which we do not take any outsiders in any part of the world into our councils on either side, there is not a state on the earth, outside of the American Union, which I like half so well as I do the state of South Carolina—[cheers]—neither England, nor Ireland, nor Scotland, nor France, nor Turkey; although from Turkey they sent me Arab horses, and from South Carolina they send me nothing but curses. Still, I like South Carolina better than I like any of them; and I have the presumption and vanity to believe that if there were nobody to overhear the state of South Carolina when she is talking, she would confess that she liked us tolerably well. I am very sure that if anybody were to make a descent on New York to-morrow—whether Louis Napoleon, or the Prince of Wales, or his mother [laughter], or the Emperor of Russia, or the Emperor of Austria, all the hills of South Carolina would pour forth their population for the rescue of New York. [Cries of "Good," and applause.] God knows how this may be. I do not pretend to know, I only conjecture. But this I do know, that if any of those powers were to make a descent on South Carolina, I know who would go to her rescue. [A voice—"We'd all go"] We would all go—everybody. ["That's so," and great applause.] Therefore they do not humbug me with their secession. [Laughter.] And I do not think they will humbug you; and I do not believe that, if they do not humbug you and me, they will much longer succeed in humbugging themselves. [Laughter.] Now, fellow-citizens, this is the ultimate result of all this business. These states are always to be together—always shall. Talk of striking down a star from that constellation. It is a thing which cannot be done. [Applause.] I do not see any less stars today than I did a week ago, and I expect to see more all the while. [Laughter.] This question then is, what in these times—when people are laboring under the delusion that they are going out of the Union and going to set up for themselves—ought we to do in order to hold them in. I do not know any better rule than the rule which every good father of a family observes. It is this. If a man wishes not to keep his family together, it is the easiest thing in the world to place them apart. He will do so at once if he only gets discontented with his son, quarrels with him, complains of him, torments him, threatens him, coerces him. This is the way to get rid of the family, and to get them all out of doors. On the other hand, if you wish to keep them, you have got only one way to do it. That is, be patient, kind, paternal, forbearing, and wait until they come to reflect for themselves. . . .

If we keep entirely cool and entirely calm, and entirely kind, a debate will ensue which will be kindly in itself, and it will prove very soon either that we are wrong—and we shall concede to our offended brethren—or else that we are right, and they will acquiesce and come back into fraternal relations with us. I do not wish to anticipate any question. We have a great many statesmen who demand at once to know what the North propose to do—what the Government proposes to do—whether we propose to coerce our southern brethren back into their allegiance. They ask us, as of course they may rightfully ask, what will be the value of fraternity which is compelled? All I have to say on that subject is, that so long ago as the time of Sir Thomas More, he discovered, and set down the discovery in his writing, that there were a great many schoolmasters, and that while there were a very few who knew how to instruct children, there were a great many who knew how to whip them. [Laughter.] I propose to have no question on that subject, but to hear complaints, to redress them if they ought to be redressed, and if we have the power to redress them; and I expect them to be withdrawn if they are unreasonable, because I know that the necessities which made this Union exist, for these states, are stronger to-day than they were when the Union was made, and that those necessities are enduring, while the passions of men are short lived and ephemeral. I believe that secession was stronger on the night of the 6th of November last, when a President and Vice-president were elected, than it is now. That is now some fifty days since, and I believe that every day's sun which set since that time, has set on mollified passions and prejudices, and that if you will only give it time, sixty days' more suns will give you a much brighter and more cheerful atmosphere. [Loud and long continued applause.]

C.

LINCOLN RULES OUT CONCESSIONS

⁋When Congress reassembled early in December, 1860, both Houses examined possible grounds for compromise between North and South. Lincoln sent confidential orders to Republican leaders in Washington to make no concessions that would weaken the party's stand against the extension of slavery into the territories either by renewal of the Missouri Compromise line or the local option principle of "popular sovereignty." The Congress could agree to no other grounds for compromise, and compromise efforts failed. (Roy P. Basler, ed., *The Collected Works of Abraham Lincoln* [New Brunswick, N.J.: Rutgers Univ. Press, 1953], IV, 149–51, 156, 158.)]

Private, & Confidential

Hon. L[yman] Trumbull.   Springfield, Ills. Dec. 10. 1860
   My dear Sir: Let there be no compromise on the question of *extending* slavery. If there be, all our labor is lost, and, ere long, must be done again. The dangerous ground—that into which some of our friends have a hankering to run—is Pop[ular] Sov[ereignty]. Have none of it. Stand firm. The tug has to come, & better now, than in any time hereafter. Yours as ever   A. LINCOLN

Private, & Confidential

Hon. William Kellogg.   Springfield, Ills.
My dear Sir—   Dec. 11, 1860
   Entertain no proposition for a compromise in regard to the *extension* of slavery. The instant you do, they have us under again; all our labor is lost, and sooner or later must be done over. Douglas is sure to be again trying to bring his "Pop. Sov." Have none of it. The tug has to come & better now than later.
   You know I think the fugitive slave clause of the constitution ought to be enforced—to put it on the mildest form, ought not to be resisted.
In haste   Yours as ever   A. LINCOLN

Private & Confidential

Hon. E[lihu] B. Washburne   Springfield, Ills.
                                                    Dec. 13. 1860
   My dear Sir. Your long letter received. Prevent, as far as possible, any of our friends from demoralizing themselves, and our cause, by entertaining propositions for compromise of any sort, on *"slavery extension"*. There is no possible compromise upon it, but which puts us under again, and leaves all our work to do over again. Whether it be a Missouri line, or Eli Thayer's Pop. Sov. it is all the same. Let either be done, & immediately filibustering and extending slavery recommences. On that point hold firm, as with a chain of steel.
          Yours as ever   A. LINCOLN

Confidential

Hon. Lyman Trumbull   Springfield, Ills.
My dear Sir.   Dec. 21, 1860

Thurlow Weed was with me nearly all day yesterday, & left at night with three short resolutions which I drew up, and which, or the substance of which, I think would do much good, if introduced, and unanimously supported by our friends. They do not touch the territorial question. Mr. Weed goes to Washington with them; and says he will, first of all, confer with you and Mr. Hamlin. I think it would be best for Mr. Seward to introduce them, & Mr. Weed will let you know that I think so. Show this to Mr. Hamlin; but beyond him, do not let my name be known in the matter. Yours as ever

A. LINCOLN

Resolutions Drawn Up for Republican Members of Senate Committee of Thirteen

[December 20, 1860]

Resolved:

That the fugitive slave clause of the Constitution ought to be enforced by a law of Congress, with efficient provisions for that object, not obliging private persons to assist in its execution, but punishing all who resist it, and with the usual safeguards to liberty, securing free men against being surrendered as slaves—

That all state laws, if there be such, really, or apparently, in conflict with such law of Congress, ought to be repealed; and no opposition to the execution of such law of Congress ought to be made—

That the Federal Union must be preserved.

D.

"THERE IS NO CRISIS"

❧President-elect Lincoln's journey from Springfield to the national capital took nearly two weeks. En route he spoke to large audiences who gathered along the railway to see the next president. Cautiously and reluctantly Lincoln occasionally touched on the secession crisis, urging his listeners to await his inaugural address for a complete statement. Meanwhile, the seven seceded states were organizing a provisional confederacy headquartered at Montgomery, Alabama. Apprehensive secessionists carefully studied Lincoln's brief speeches for clues to his attitudes toward secession and coercion. As events later proved, Lincoln grossly misjudged the secession crisis when he declared, *"There is no crisis,* excepting such a one as may be gotten up at any time by designing politicians," and he overestimated the degree of Union sentiment in the cotton states. (Basler, *The Collected Works of Abraham Lincoln,* IV, 195–96, 207, 211, 215–16.)]

Speech from the Balcony of the Bates House at Indianapolis, Indiana

February 11, 1861

. . . THE WORDS "coercion" and "invasion" are in great use about these days. Suppose we, were simply to try if we can, and ascertain what, is the meaning of these words. Let us get, if we can, the exact definitions of these words—not from dictionaries, but from the men who constantly repeat them—what things they mean to express by the words. What, then, is "coercion"? What is "invasion"? Would the marching of an army into South Carolina, for instance, without the consent of her people, and in hostility against them, be coercion or invasion? I very frankly say, I think it would be invasion, and it would be coercion too, if the people of that country were forced to submit. But if the Government, for instance, but simply insists upon holding its own forts, or retaking those forts which belong to it,—[cheers,]— or the enforcement of the laws of the United States in the collection of duties upon foreign importations—[renewed cheers,]—or even the withdrawal of the mails from those portions of the country where the mails themselves are habitually violated; would any or all of these things be coercion? Do the lovers of the Union contend that they will resist coercion or invasion of any State, understanding that any or all of these would be coercing or invading a State? If they do, then it occurs to me that the means for the preservation of the Union they so greatly love, in their own estimation, is of a very thin and airy charac- ter. [Applause.] If sick, they would consider the little pills of the homoepathist as already too large for them to swallow. In their view, the Union, as a family relation, would not be anything like a regular marriage at all, but only as a sort of free-love arrangement,—[laughter,] —to be maintained on what that sect calls passionate attraction. [Con- tinued laughter.] But, my friends, enough of this.

What is the particular sacredness of a State? I speak not of that position which is given to a State in and by the Constitution of the United States, for that all of us agree to—we abide by; but that posi- tion assumed, that a State can carry it out of the Union that which it holds in sacredness by virtue of its connection with the Union. I am speaking of that assumed right of a State, as a primary principle, that the Constitution should rule all that is less than itself, and ruin all that is bigger than itself. [Laughter.] But, I ask, wherein does consist that right? If a State, in one instance, and a county in another, should be equal in extent of territory, and equal in the number of people, wherein is that State any better than the county? Can a change of name change the right? By what principle of original right is it that one-fiftieth or one-ninetieth of a great nation, by calling themselves a State, have the right to break up and ruin that nation as a matter of original principle? Now, I ask the question—I am not deciding anything—[laughter,]— and with the request that you will think somewhat upon that subject and decide for yourselves, if you choose, when you get ready,—where is the mysterious, original right, from principle, for a certain district of country with inhabitants, by merely being called a State, to play tyrant over all its own citizens, and deny .the authority of everything greater than itself. [Laughter.] I say I am deciding nothing, but simply giving something for you to reflect upon; and, with having said this much, and having declared, in the start, that I will make no long speeches, I thank you again for this magnificent welcome, and bid you an affectionate farewell. [Cheers.]

Speech at Steubenville, Ohio

February 14, 1861

. . . We everywhere express devotion to the Constitution. I believe there is no difference in this respect, whether on this or on the other side of this majestic stream. I understand that on the other side, among our dissatisfied brethren, they are satisfied with the Constitution of the United States, if they can have their rights under the Constitution. The question is, as to what the Constitution means—"What are their rights under the Constitution?" That is all. To decide that, who shall be the judge? Can you think of any other, than the voice of the people? If the majority does not control, the minority must—would that be right? Would that be just or generous? Assuredly not! Though the majority may be wrong, and I will not undertake to say that they were not wrong in electing me, yet we must adhere to the principle that the majority shall rule. By your Constitution you have another change in four years. No great harm can be done by us in that time—in that time there can be nobody hurt. If anything goes wrong, however, and you find you have made a mistake, elect a better man next time. There are plenty of them.

(Here the Engine whistled.) These points involve the discussion of many questions which I have not time to consider. I merely give them to you for your reflection. I almost regret that I alluded to it at all.

Ladies, gentlemen and friends, I thank you for this kind and overwhelming reception, and bid you farewell.

Speech at Pittsburgh, Pennsylvania

February 15, 1861

. . . Notwithstanding the troubles across the river, [the speaker pointing southwardly, and smiling] there is really no crisis, springing from anything in the government itself. In plain words, there is really no crisis except an *artificial one!* What is there now to warrant the condition of affairs presented by our friends "over the river?" Take even their own view of the questions involved, and there is nothing to justify the course which they are pursuing. I repeat it, then—*there is no crisis*, excepting such a one as may be gotten up at any time by designing politicians. My advice, then, under such circumstances, is to keep cool. If the great American people will only keep their temper, on both sides of the line, the troubles will come to an end, and the question which now distracts the country will be settled just as surely as all other difficulties of like character which have originated in this government have been adjusted. Let the people on both sides keep their self-possession, and just as other clouds have cleared away in due time, so will this, and this great nation shall continue to prosper as heretofore. . . .

Speech at Cleveland, Ohio

February 15, 1861

. . . Frequent allusion is made to the excitement at present existing in our national politics, and it is as well that I should also allude to it here. I think that there is no occasion for any excitement. The crisis, as it is called, is altogether an artificial crisis. In all parts of the nation there are differences of opinion and politics. There are differences of opinion even here. You did not all vote in the person who now addresses you. What is happening now will not hurt those who are farther away from here. Have they not all their rights now as they ever have had? Do they not have their fugitive slaves returned now as ever? Have they not the same constitution that they have lived under for seventy odd years? Have they not a position as citizens of this common country, and have we any power to change that position? (Cries of "No.") What then is the matter with them? Why all this excitement? Why all these complaints? As I said before, this crisis is all artificial. It has no foundation in facts. It was not argued up, as the saying is, and cannot, therefore, be argued down. Let it alone and it will go down by itself (Laughter). . . .

E.

"THE UNION IS UNBROKEN"

⟪President Lincoln's inaugural address on March 4, 1861, indicated that the new administration would not recognize secession, but that for the time being it would act with forbearance toward the cotton states. Lincoln hoped that time would prove both the folly of disunion and the good will of his administration toward all sections of the country. Addressing himself to those "who really love the Union," he appealed for a calm re-examination of the consequences of disunion. Neither side conceded, and six weeks later the war that both deprecated began. The secession issue was to be resolved on the battlefield at a cost that no man could predict. (Richardson, *A Compilation of the Messages and Papers of the Presidents,* VI, 6–12.)

What arguments did Lincoln use to prove his case against secession? What alternatives did he hold out to the seceding states? How did Lincoln's policy differ from Buchanan's? Compare Lincoln's and Buchanan's views of the nature of the Union.]

FELLOW-CITIZENS of the United States. . . . It is seventy-two years since the first inauguration of a President under our National Constitution. During that period fifteen different and greatly distinguished citizens have in succession administered the executive branch of the Government. They have conducted it through many perils, and generally with great success. Yet, with all this scope of precedent, I now enter upon the same task for the brief constitutional term of four years under great and peculiar difficulty. A disruption of the Federal Union, heretofore only menaced, is now formidably attempted.

I hold that in contemplation of universal law and of the Constitution the Union of these States is perpetual. Perpetuity is implied, if not expressed, in the fundamental law of all national governments. It is safe to assert that no government proper ever had a provision in its organic law for its own termination. Continue to execute all the express provisions of our National Constitution, and the Union will endure forever, it being impossible to destroy except by some action not provided for in the instrument itself. . . .

I therefore consider that in view of the Constitution and the laws the Union is unbroken, and to the extent of my ability I shall take care, as the Constitution itself expressly enjoins me, that the laws of the Union be faithfully executed in all the States. Doing this I deem to be only a simple duty on my part, and I shall perform it so far as practicable unless my rightful masters, the American people, shall withhold the requisite means or in some authoritative manner direct the contrary. I trust this will not be regarded as a menace, but only as the declared purpose of the Union that it *will* constitutionally defend and maintain itself.

In doing this there needs to be no bloodshed or violence, and there shall be none unless it be forced upon the national authority. The power confided to me will be used to hold, occupy, and possess the property and places belonging to the Government and to collect the duties and imposts; but beyond what may be necessary for these objects, there will be no invasion, no using of force against or among the people anywhere. Where hostility to the United States in any interior locality shall be so great and universal as to prevent competent resident citizens from holding the Federal offices, there will be no attempt to force obnoxious strangers among the people for that object. While the strict legal right may exist in the Government to enforce the exercise of these offices, the attempt to do so would be so irritating and so nearly impracticable withal that I deem it better to forego for the time the uses of such offices.

The mails, unless repelled, will continue to be furnished in all parts of the Union. So far as possible the people everywhere shall have that sense of perfect security which is most favorable to calm thought and reflection. The course here indicated will be followed unless current events and experience shall show a modification or change to be proper, and in every case and exigency my best discretion will be exercised, according to circumstances actually existing and with a view and a hope of a peaceful solution of the national troubles and the restoration of fraternal sympathies and affections.

That there are persons in one section or another who seek to destroy the Union at all events and are glad of any pretext to do it I will neither affirm nor deny; but if there be such, I need address no word to them. To those, however, who really love the Union may I not speak?

Before entering upon so grave a matter as the destruction of our national fabric, with all its benefits, its memories, and its hopes, would it not be wise to ascertain precisely why we do it? Will you hazard so desperate a step while there is any possibility that any portion of the ills you fly from have no real existence? Will you, while the certain ills you fly to are greater than all the real ones you fly from, will you risk the commission of so fearful a mistake?

All profess to be content in the Union if all constitutional rights can be maintained. Is it true, then, that any right plainly written in the Constitution has been denied? I think not. Happily, the human mind is so constituted that no party can reach to the audacity of doing this. Think, if you can, of a single instance in which a plainly written provision of the Constitution has ever been denied. If by the mere force of numbers a majority should deprive a minority of any clearly written constitutional right, it might in a moral point of view justify revolution; certainly would if such right were a vital one. But such is not our case. All the vital rights of minorities and of individuals are so plainly assured to them by affirmations and negations, guaranties and prohibitions, in the Constitution that controversies never arise concerning them. . . .

Plainly the central idea of secession is the essence of anarchy. A majority held in restraint by constitutional checks and limitations, and always changing easily with deliberate changes of popular opinions and sentiments, is the only true sovereign of a free people. Whoever rejects it does of necessity fly to anarchy or to despotism. Unanimity is impossible. The rule of a minority, as a permanent arrangement, is wholly inadmissible; so that, rejecting the majority principle, anarchy or despotism in some form is all that is left. . . .

One section of our country believes slavery is *right* and ought to be extended, while the other believes it is *wrong* and ought not to be extended. This is the only substantial dispute. The fugitive-slave clause of the Constitution and the law for the suppression of the foreign slave trade are each as well enforced, perhaps, as any law can ever be in a community where the moral sense of the people imperfectly supports the law itself. The great body of the people abide by the dry legal obligation in both cases, and a few break over in each. This, I think, can not be perfectly cured, and it would be worse in both cases *after* the separation of the sections than before. The foreign slave trade, now imperfectly suppressed, would be ultimately revived without restriction in one section, while fugitive slaves, now only partially surrendered, would not be surrendered at all by the other.

Physically speaking, we can not separate. We can not remove our respective sections from each other nor build an impassable wall between them. A husband and wife may be divorced and go out of the presence and beyond the reach of each other, but the different parts of our country can not do this. They can not but remain face to face, and intercourse, either amicable or hostile, must continue between them. Is it possible, then, to make that intercourse more advantageous or more satisfactory *after* separation than *before*? Can aliens make treaties easier than friends can make laws? Can treaties be more faithfully enforced between aliens than laws can among friends? Suppose you go to war, you can not fight always; and when, after much loss on both sides and no gain on either, you cease fighting, the identical old questions, as to terms of intercourse, are again upon you.

This country, with its institutions, belongs to the people who inhabit it. Whenever they shall grow weary of the existing Government, they can exercise their *constitutional* right of amending it or their *revolutionary* right to dismember or overthrow it. I can not be ignorant of the fact that many worthy and patriotic citizens are desirous of having the National Constitution amended. While I make no recommendation of amendments, I fully recognize the rightful authority of the people over the whole subject, to be exercised in either of the modes prescribed in the instrument itself; and I should, under existing circumstances, favor rather than oppose a fair opportunity being afforded the people to act upon it. I will venture to add that to me the convention mode seems preferable, in that it allows amendments to originate with the people themselves, instead of only permitting them to take or reject propositions originated by others, not especially chosen for the purpose, and which might not be precisely such as they would wish to either accept or refuse. I understand a proposed amendment to the Constitution—which amendment, however, I have not seen—has passed Congress, to the effect that the Federal Government shall never interfere with the domestic institutions of the States, including that of persons held to service. To avoid misconstruction of what I have said, I depart from my purpose not to speak of particular amendments so far as to say that, holding such a provision to now be implied constitutional law, I have no objection to it being made express and irrevocable.

The Chief Magistrate derives all his authority from the people, and they have conferred none upon him to fix terms for the separation of the States. The people themselves can do this also if they choose, but the Executive as such has nothing to do with it. His duty is to administer the present Government as it came to his hands and to transmit it unimpaired by him to his successor.

Why should there not be a patient confidence in the ultimate justice of the people? Is there any better or equal hope in the world? In our present differences, is either party without faith of being in the right? If the Almighty Ruler of Nations, with His eternal truth and justice, be on your side of the North, or on yours of the South, that truth and that justice will surely prevail by the judgment of this great tribunal of the American people.

By the frame of the Government under which we live this same people have wisely given their public servants but little power for mischief, and have with equal wisdom provided for the return of that little to their own hands at very short intervals. While the people retain their virtue and vigilance no Administration by any extreme of wickedness or folly can very seriously injure the Government in the short space of four years.

My countrymen, one and all, think calmly and *well* upon this whole subject. Nothing valuable can be lost by taking time. If there be an object to *hurry* any of you in hot haste to a step which you would never take *deliberately*, that object will be frustrated by taking time; but no good object can be frustrated by it. Such of you as are now dissatisfied still have the old Constitution unimpaired, and, on the sensitive point, the laws of your own framing under it; while the new Administration will have no immediate power, if it would, to change either. If it were admitted that you who are dissatisfied hold the right side in the dispute, there still is no single good reason for precipitate action. Intelligence, patriotism, Christianity, and a firm reliance on Him who has never yet forsaken this favored land are still competent to adjust in the best way all our present difficulty.

In *your* hands, my dissatisfied fellow-countrymen, and not in *mine*, is the momentous issue of civil war. The Government will not assail *you*. You can have no conflict without being yourselves the aggressors. *You* have no oath registered in heaven to destroy the Government, while *I* shall have the most solemn one to "preserve, protect, and defend it."

I am loath to close. We are not enemies, but friends. We must not be enemies. Though passion may have strained it must not break our bonds of affection. The mystic chords of memory, stretching from every battlefield and patriot grave to every living heart and hearthstone all over this broad land, will yet swell the chorus of the Union, when again touched, as surely they will be, by the better angels of our nature.

FOR FURTHER READING

Dwight L. Dumond, *The Secession Movement, 1860–1861* (New York: Macmillan, 1931) and Allan Nevins, *The Emergence of Lincoln* (New York: Scribner's, 1950), II, chapters 7–15, are the best general accounts of this period. Bruce Catton, *The Coming Fury* (Volume I of the *Centennial History* of the *Civil War*, New York: Doubleday, 1961), chapters 1–5, is a fine popular account. Dwight L. Dumond, *Southern Editorials on Secession* (New York: Century, 1931) and Howard Cecil Perkins, *Northern Editorials on Secession* (New York: Appleton-Century-Crofts, Inc., 1942) are good supplementary sources.

There are several studies of the secession movement and its leaders in particular states. The more useful are Percy L. Rainwater, *Mississippi, Storm Center of Secession, 1850–1861* (Baton Rouge, La.: Claitor's Book Store, 1938); Clarence P. Denman, *The Secession Movement in Alabama* (Montgomery: Alabama State College Department of Archives and History, 1933); Henry T. Shanks, *The Secession Movement in Virginia, 1847–1861* (Richmond: Garrett, 1934); and Laura A. White, *Robert Barnwell Rhett: Father of Secession* (New York: Century, 1931).

David M. Potter, *Lincoln and His Party in the Secession Crisis* (New Haven: Yale Univ. Press, 1942) and Kenneth M. Stampp, *And the War Came; The North and the Secession Crisis, 1860–1861* (Baton Rouge: Louisiana State Univ. Press, 1950) discuss the Republican party's response to secession. Roy F. Nichols, *The Disruption of the American Democracy* (New York: Macmillan, 1948), chapters XX–XXVII, summarizes Buchanan's difficulties in meeting the crisis.